SHELLEY POTTERIES

SHELLEY POTTERIES

*The History and Production of
a Staffordshire Family of Potters*

Chris Watkins
William Harvey
Robert Senft

BARRIE & JENKINS
London Melbourne Auckland Johannesburg

First published in 1980 by Barrie & Jenkins, an imprint of
Century Hutchinson Ltd.,
Brookmount House, 62-65 Chandos Place,
Covent Garden, London WC2N 4NW.

Century Hutchinson Publishing Group (Australia) Pty Ltd
16-22 Church Street, Hawthorn, Melbourne, Victoria 3122.

Century Hutchinson Group (NZ) Ltd.,
32-34 View Road, P O Box 40-086, Glenfield, Auckland 10.

Century Hutchinson Group (SA) Pty Ltd.,
P O Box 337, Bergvlei 2012, South Africa.

Reprinted under licence from Ebury Press in 1994 by
Forsyth Consultancy Limited
Richmond, Surrey TW10 5BB

Printed and bound in Great Britain by
Bookcraft Ltd.,
Midsomer Norton, Bath, Avon BA3 2BX.

Monochrome plate enhancement by
Acegraphics Ltd.,
Richmond, Surrey TW9 1RJ.

British Library Cataloguing in Publication Data

Watkins, Chris
Shelley Potteries :   the history and
production of a Staffordshire family
of potters
  1.   Shelley Potteries --- History

Rn: Harvey, William Pettit I. Title
     II. Harvey, William, 1949-
     III.   Senft, Robert

388.7'6663942463   HD9612.9.S/

ISBN   0 09 1432707

Contents

		page
	Preface and acknowledgements	7
	List of plates	9
	Introduction	13
1	Shelleys' early background in the Potteries	15
2	The history of the Foley Works	18
3	Shelleys and Wileman & Co.	21
4	Into the twentieth century	50
5	Post-war developments	63
6	A pottery named Shelleys	79
7	A high-point in style	93
8	Advertising, promotion and display	114
9	Shelleys' production techniques	127
10	The war years, 1939–45, and their aftermath	133
11	Modernization and take-over	146
	Epilogue	163
	Appendix A: Backstamps	164
	Appendix B: Pattern numbers	166
	Appendix C: Registered design numbers	169
	Appendix D: A chronology of the firm	171
	Bibliography	172
	Index	173

Preface and acknowledgements

The story of the Shelley Potteries could not have been written without the active assistance of many people. The prime reason for this is that the pottery, which was active up to 1966, did not leave behind the sort of archives which some of the larger firms possess, nor did any organized records survive the various take-overs and reorganizations since that date. The small section of pottery history which this book records, then, is the result of a 'reconstruction' task from a wide range of sources. We are happy to acknowledge below those people concerned.

We owe particular thanks to Paul Atterbury and Louise Irvine of the Royal Doulton historical department; without their considerable advice and continuous support we can confidently state this book would not have been written. We are indebted to the former art director, Eric Slater, who has given freely his time and recollections, as have other former employees. Also our thanks go to the present-day members of the Shelley family – Alan and Sue, Donald and Val, Eileen, Doris – they have stood up well to our pestering and have provided significant information. We are very grateful to a number of individuals who have made available for photography items from their collections – Paul Smith, Jeanette Young, Robert Brown, Peter Chapman, Mike Hougham, Margaret Caistor, Roy Mance, Toby Andersen, Johny Lochtie, John Evans and John Wickham; without them this book would have looked much poorer. That comment applies with greater force to our creative colour photographer, Brian

Bates, who has shown endless patience in the face of our complex demands. Several of the black and white photographs were taken by Moira Walters and Philip de Bay. Our typist, Caroline Wilkinson, has played an important part by making our text readable.

Our gratitude also goes to the helpful staff and individuals at the following institutions: City Museum of Stoke-on-Trent, Minton Museum, Rodney Hampson and the Gladstone Pottery Museum, Wedgwood Museum, Menai Museum of Childhood, Jennifer Hawkins at the Victoria & Albert Museum, National Art Library, British Museum Library, Horace Barks Reference Library at Hanley, Science Reference Library, University of London Library, University of Keele Library, Sylvia Katz at the Design Council, Design Registry, Public Records Office, and Tableware International. Horace Barks Reference Library, University of London, Design Council, Design Registry and the Science Reference Library also kindly gave permission to reproduce photographs.

None of the above can, of course, be held responsible for the inaccuracies in our text which will no doubt come to light – we claim full responsibility.

A final thank-you goes to the staff of the following museums who have assisted with the travelling exhibition of Shelley wares which we have mounted in conjunction with this book: Geffrye Museum, London; City Museum, Stoke-on-Trent; Lotherton Hall, Leeds; City Museum, Bristol; and Huntly House Museum, Edinburgh.

One last prefacing note addressed to all those other enthusiasts who have at some time contemplated writing a book on their favourite objects – it can be done!

List of plates

Colour

between pages 56 and 57

I   Intarsio ware by Frederick Rhead, 1897–9
II   Umbrella stands and an advertising tile, c. 1900
III   Clock cases, c. 1897–1900
IV   Intarsio ware, second series, by Walter Slater, 1911–15
V   Lustre wares by Walter Slater, c. 1919–21
VI   The Shelley Girl advertising figure, c. 1925
VII   (a) Queen Anne shape coffee sets, 1928 and 1927
     (b) Queen Anne shape teaware, 1927–9
VIII (a) Nursery teaset by Mabel Lucie Attwell, 1926
     (b) Nursery teaset by Hilda Cowham, 1928

between pages 104 and 105

IX   Selection of figures by Mabel Lucie Attwell, from 1937
X   (a) Vogue shape teaset and coffee set, 1930
     (b) Vogue shape dinnerware, 1930
XI   Mode shape coffee cups, Mode and Vogue shape teacups, 1930
XII Regent shape teaware, 1932–4
XIII Tea, coffee and dinner set in Regent shape, 1933
XIV (a) Tea and coffee ware in Eve shape, 1932
     (b) Assorted Harmony Artware, 1932–9

XV   Selection of Harmony Artware, 1932–9
XVI   Tankards with sgraffito-groundlay decoration by Eric Slater,
      c. 1951

Monochrome

		page
1	J. B. Shelley (1836–96)	14
2	Advertisement for J. F. Wileman earthenware works, 1881	19
3	Teaware, ribbed shape 1886, blue pattern 1888	23
4	Dainty White teaware by Rowland Morris, 1896	25
5	Intarsio pattern 3165, c. 1899	31
6	Ewers in Intarsio ware, 1898	32
7	Variety of Intarsio pieces, 1899	33
8	Intarsio ware, Shakespeare style, c. 1900	33
9	Intarsio teapot depicting Lord Salisbury, 1900	35
10	Two vases showing the sgraffito technique	36
11	Jug with Urbato decoration, 1898	36
12	Variety of Urbato ware, 1899	37
13	Design for a vase by Frederick Rhead, 1897	38
14	Wileman & Co. factory view, c. 1900	39
15	Design for a grotesque by Frederick Rhead, 1899	40
16	Grotesques and jugs, 1899	41
17	Toilet set by Frederick Rhead, 1897	42
18	Sgraffito ware by Frederick Rhead, c. 1900	42
19	Later designs by Frederick Rhead, c. 1902	43
20	Illustration from *Pilgrim's Progress*, 1898	44
21	Liberty's Christmas catalogue cover, 1893	45
22	Poster by Louis Rhead, 1896	46
23	Photograph of Frederick Rhead, 1922	48
24	Lactolian ware vase by Walter Slater, c. 1902	55
25	Intarsio ware, second series, by Walter Slater, 1911	57
26	Toilet sets, c. 1915	58
27	Ashbourne pattern on china, 1913	60
28	Bowl and vases with Roself and Violette decorations, 1915–16	61
29	Factory view (from 1950)	64
30	Heraldic china from a catalogue, 1922	67

31 Heraldic china from a catalogue, 1922   68
32 Commemorative pieces, 1897–1936   70
33 Commemorative wares from 1937   70
34 Lustre, floating flower bowls and a spill jar, with teaware,
    1920   72
35 Oriental-style decanter, 1915   74
36 Indian Peony pattern on earthenware and china, c. 1918   76
37 Jack and Eileen, Bob and Doris at their wedding, 1923   77
38 Nursery ware by Mabel Lucie Attwell, 1926   81
39 Nursery ware by Hilda Cowham, 1927   82
40 Mabel Lucie Attwell Animal series, 1930   83
41 Mabel Lucie Attwell chamberpot, mug and baby plate,
    c. 1934   84
42 Advertisement for jelly moulds, 1925   86
43 Twelve jelly mould shapes, 1922   87
44 Advertising ware, c. 1912–34   89
45 Photograph of Percy Shelley, c. 1930   90
46 Bob, Jack, Percy and Norman at the works, c. 1930   91
47 Queen Anne shape teaware, 1928   95
48 Shelley pieces in the style of W. Moorcroft, c. 1929   97
49 Walter Slater, Eric Slater and Clara Knight, c. 1930   98
50 Patterns for the Mode shape, 1930   99
51 Coffee sets in the Mode shape, 1930   100
52 Teaset in the Eve shape, 1932   100
53 Dinnerware in the Eve shape, 1934   103
54 Breakfast set in Swirls pattern, 1934   105
55 Earthenware lamp bases, c. 1936   108
56 Harmony ware catalogue cover, c. 1934   111
57 Detail from advertising leaflet, 1926   116
58 Advertising umbrella stand, c. 1926   116
59 Shelley Girl advertisement, 1926   117
60 Shelley Girl, the Shelley Standard, 1927   117
61 Advertisement for Vogue shape teaware, 1931   119
62 Example of a window display, 1931   120
63 Detail from one of Smedley's advertisements, 1936   123
64 John Sayer's 'Uniservice' stand, 1934   125
65 Placing the 'green' ware into saggars, c. 1930   128
66 Creating bungs of saggars in the bisque oven, c. 1930   129
67 Making transfers from copper-plate engravings, c. 1930   131
68 The decorating shop and enamellers, c. 1930   131

69 Dinnerware from the Britain Can Make It exhibition,
      1946   139
70 Advertisement for export ware   140
71 Bowl by Eric Slater shown at the Festival of Britain   143
72 Dinner plate and soup bowl, 1951   144
73 Lustre bowls by Eric Slater, 1953   149
74 Donald Shelley with one of the 'Top Hat' kilns   151
75 Bowl of experimental design by Eric Slater, c. 1954   154
76 Experimental design by Eric Slater, 1955   154
77 The Stirling coupe shape, 1956   157
78 Tea and coffee ware in the Avon shape, 1965   161

Introduction

We believe that the Shelley story deserves to be told for a number of reasons. First, as a record of the history and activity of the Shelley pottery we have tried to make this work informative, comprehensive and accurate: in this way we hope to be of service to collectors and others interested in this particular company. Second, as a pottery catering for public tastes Shelley can be seen as illustrating the changes in style and design from the 1880s to the 1960s. At the time of writing, the name of Shelley is most often connected with the styles of the 1930s: we are glad to be able to show equally striking wares from other periods and sometimes to hypothesize about the influences affecting designers. The third reason for telling this story is that the Shelley pottery can be seen as representative of many other relatively small firms in the Stoke-on-Trent area. With its roots dating back to the rise of the Staffordshire potteries, this family business is like many others which flourished in the first half of this century, only to be lost in larger conglomerations in the second half as a result of modern technology and industrial rationalization. We have attempted to place the production of Shelley wares into their social and economic context, where possible, so that design is not considered in abstract.

The history of the family, the pottery and the wares produced is told for the most part in chronological order and includes information on the family histories of the art directors. A whole chapter is devoted to the advertising and display of the 1920s and 1930s as this was a particularly prominent feature.

I

Shelleys' early background in the Potteries

The name of Shelley is generally associated with china and pottery of the twentieth century, but one should not begin by assuming that the roots of the enterprise described in this book were not based in the much earlier period of pottery history which saw the rise of the Staffordshire potteries.

A number of generations of the Shelley family were recorded in Lane End from the middle of the eighteenth century. In those times Lane End – previously Meir Lane End – was a small settlement where lands had become available for lesser potters to acquire a site, in contrast to the larger businesses in Burslem which had been established for some time. It was at Lane End that the manufacture of china was to become a speciality, possibly because the local coal provided the high temperature required for firing bone china. The growth of this trade was to turn this small crossroads village into the thriving town of Longton, the official change of name taking place in 1848.

The first recorded potter in the family was Randle Shelley (1706–81) who is reported to have been carrying out his trade in 1748. Although little is known of his works or his wares, his was probably a prosperous concern for in 1774 his two sons Michael (1744–88) and Thomas (1746–98) bought land on which they set up two separate businesses. From these adjoining sites, on one of which the Gladstone Pottery Museum has recently been established, the Shelleys developed a thriving trade. They produced their own earthenware plates and dishes and numbered among their customers Josiah Wedgwood at Etruria. A bill

1 J. B. Shelley (1836–96)

from Thomas Shelley to Mr Wedgwood dated May 1787 shows over
five thousand pieces to have been delivered for the princely sum of
£29 14s. (£29.70), an average rate of nearly 1½d. (½p) per item. It
would seem that some of the work done was intricate, with Wedgwood
paying nearly 11d. (4½p) for some oval dishes. Probably these were
sold again by Wedgwood to those of his customers who required plain
creamwares. The numbering of crates suggests that many such orders
had been supplied previously. Michael died in 1788 and his works
were sold to a neighbour for £900, but two years later Thomas bought
back the smaller pottery and worked both concerns. He was to become
an important figure in Lane End: a churchwarden, a trustee of the rebuilding of the church, and the owner of a large farm nearby. When
he died in 1798 the works were sold, items at the sale including 1,100
saggars and 300 workboards – an indication of the large scale of the
Shelley business. Indeed, from what little evidence is available it could
be inferred that Thomas Shelley was a man of substance and was
credited as such by his contemporaries in potting – possibly unusual
for a Lane End man amongst the old-established families. He was a
member of the Committee of Commerce for the Potteries from its
inauguration in 1784, and was entrusted (along with others) with the
task of going to Devon 'to lease clay'. In 1790 he was one element of a
partnership, with Josiah Spode the younger, and eleven other potters,
aimed at securing that other important raw material, coal, from local
mines.

Of the next generation it is difficult to create a clear picture. One of
Michael's sons, John (b. 1778), may have been the John Shelley who
in 1799 made a small mould depicting a master potter at work. It is
thought to represent William Turner of the famous Turner's factory
of Lane End, together with his apprentice turning the wheel, and shows
considerable detail, some of which suggests that the potter was also
a member of the local Volunteer force. This earthenware mould is now
in the Spode Museum, and an enamelled plaque, also signed by John
Shelley and possibly taken from the mould, is in the City Museum,
Stoke-on-Trent.

Of Thomas's children, the eldest son Thomas (1776–1804), seems
to have become a potter at Lane Delph just a few miles from the site of
his father's works and very close to the spot where twentieth-century
Shelley wares were made. However, he seems to have been unsuccessful
there; he was declared bankrupt earlier in the year of his death.
Another son, William (1786–1841), appears to have returned to carry

on his father's factory under the title of Shelley, Pye & Company from 1812–21 and other members of the family lived at the house adjoining the works.

It was through the son Thomas, however, that the family descendants created the twentieth-century enterprise. After his marriage to Ann Bolton in 1799, their only son Thomas Bolton Shelley (1802–40) was born. He was orphaned at the age of two, but maintained the family's connection with potting, as he was brought up by the William Shelley mentioned above. It was Thomas Bolton Shelley who, after marrying Eliza Ball in 1835, became the father of the man who eventually entered into a partnership which gave rise to the firm as it is now known. Joseph Ball Shelley was born in 1836, grew up in Longton, and by the age of fifteen had become an attorney's clerk. His father had died when he was four years of age and his step-father, Samuel Hartshorne, was working in partnership with the pottery firm of Ferneyhough & Adams at the Dresden Works, Stafford Street, Longton. In 1853 James Ferneyhough left the partnership and it appears that in 1854 Hartshorne also left, leaving John Adams in sole charge. However, by 1858 the works had passed into the hands of Shelley and Hartshorne, who produced the 'usual varieties of services in china of a good quality' (Jewitt, 1878). No information is available regarding a trademark for this enterprise, and in fact the partnership only lasted until 1861, to be succeeded by a partnership between Joseph Shelley, James Adams and Harvey Adams. Trading under the name of Shelley & Adams, this too was a short-lived enterprise: in 1862 J. B. Shelley's connection with the Dresden Works was terminated and the pottery returned to the Ferneyhough family by 1866. Again, it is unlikely that a Shelley & Adams trademark existed on the china produced.

2

The history of the Foley Works

With regard to the background of the Shelley enterprise which carried on into the twentieth century, it is necessary to focus attention on an area between Fenton and Longton which is known as the Foley. The name derives from the Foley family who owned property in the neighbourhood, and survives to this day in Foley Street and the Foley Arms.

From the 1820s the firm of Elkin, Knight & Co. had produced earthenwares at a factory called the Foley Potteries which was built in about 1820. During a succession of partnerships blue-printed wares were made, including Willow pattern, Broseley pattern, Canton Views and Pennsylvania. By 1853 John King Knight was sole proprietor, and he decided to take into partnership Mr Henry Wileman, an event of great importance to the Shelley family in later years. At that time Joseph Shelley was working in one of the numerous partnerships that failed, and the Foley Potteries also seemed in a relatively unstable condition: this state of affairs may have been caused by a lack of capital, an important consideration at a time when more mechanized processes were being introduced to the developing industry. Financial backing was therefore very important – a partner with capital was particularly valuable.

Henry Wileman (1798–1864) had been a glass and Staffordshire-ware dealer in Paddington, had owned a china warehouse in London's Edgware Road, and at one time became owner of the Church Gresley Pottery, Derbyshire. After three years of trading as Knight & Wileman, J. K. Knight retired and Henry Wileman traded under his own name.

It seems likely that business was successful, for in 1860 he built the Foley China Works alongside the Foley Potteries. It was in the former of these that the ware later marked Shelley would be produced.

The two factories stretched along the main Longton-to-Fenton road but were some distance back from it. They were separated by a private road and at a later date were joined by a bridge (see plate 14 showing the expanded china works in about 1900). Originally, the china works consisted of a single quadrangle of three-storey buildings which opened on to the private road. Five kilns were incorporated, these having the classical shape which gives them their names – bottle ovens. The earthenware works illustrated in plate 2 included four glost and four bisque ovens towards the rear of the main buildings. As can be seen, they were connected by a spur line to the goods railway which in turn connected Longton with Stoke Wharf and which had been opened in 1805 to counteract Longton's problem of having no canal.

Two years after the Foley China Works were built, J. B. Shelley left the Dresden Works and in the same year joined Henry Wileman in the capacity of traveller for the firm. In 1864 Henry Wileman died, leaving the business to be run by his sons, James F. and Charles J. Wileman. This was to last only two years, after which the interests were divided, James managing the earthenware works and Charles managing the china works. However, Charles retired from the enterprise in 1870, leaving James as proprietor of both works.

It seems that in this period the new china works had not yet created a significant reputation: by 1878 L. Jewitt wrote, 'the china produced is of the ordinary useful class for household purposes'. Plain white china or with gold line borders is reported to have been made. Meanwhile the earthenware works, Foley Potteries, were producing printed

2 Advertisement for J. F. Wileman earthenware works, 1881

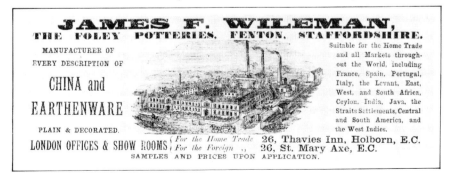

wares, lustres, cream-coloured and granite wares. It may have been the case that James Wileman had a greater interest in earthenware manufacture, for when he took Joseph Shelley into partnership in 1872 this association appears to have covered only the china works. Indeed, twelve years later James Wileman retired from the china works to manage solely the earthenware until that factory closed with his retirement in 1892. Today the front buildings of the old earthenware works still stretch along the main road, while the rear area has been taken over by a bone-milling concern.

Thus, when the Shelley family first became formally associated with the works which would later carry their name, Joseph Shelley became proprietor of a factory which had some features recognizable in modern industrial concerns. Export trade was of great importance: competitors such as the U.S.A. and Germany had caught up with Britain's advances in mechanical invention and the battle for world trade was strong. Wileman's advertised their wares as 'suitable for all markets throughout the world', listing countries which included the Levant and Java, but which omitted Germany and North America. Showrooms and agents in London had been set up, separate ones for home trade and foreign trade, but both in the Holborn area of London, which was then the centre of china, pottery and glass showrooms.

Other less attractive features of factories developed, however, for it was beginning to be recognized that this particular method of organizing production also led to problems of unemployment, and the great growth of factories, with the associated drift of population from the country to the towns, brought with it the growth of slum housing and similar modern difficulties. Other aspects of the new works could not be regarded as modern. Workers were campaigning for a fifty-four-hour week, which might allow Saturday afternoons free. Hours of work were generally between 6 a.m. and 6 p.m. and the recent Education Act of 1870 meant that children could now only work half of these hours. Transport was either horse-powered by road or by canal – the 1865 'Man and Flag' Act, requiring vehicles driven by mechanical power to be preceded by a man waving a red flag, had yet to be repealed.

3

Shelleys and Wileman & Co.

When Joseph Shelley became partner to James Wileman in 1872, the name of the Foley China Works became Wileman & Co. (sometimes James Wileman & Co. in the initial stages) and was to remain so for over fifty years, even though Wileman severed his connection after twelve. The influence of the Shelley family was consolidated in 1881 when Joseph's son Percy joined the business.

Percy Shelley was born in Longton in 1860 but could not be described as having been born and bred in the home of the china industry. He had received a boarding-school education, going on to attend Owen's College, Manchester, and had gained a B.A. degree from London University. These experiences, which were becoming more commonplace for boys of middle-class families, may have had an effect on Percy's attitude towards the business he entered. He appears to have had a definite wish to create pottery and china which was of higher quality than the average, something which was a cut above the rest. Although he did not receive a formal training in pottery, Percy Shelley was to become known first and foremost as a potter, and during his fifty years as head of the firm he was to develop the lasting reputation of Shelley china.

In the 1880s the wares produced could not reasonably be described as outstanding. The body, that is, the combination of clays and other ingredients which made up the china, was of average quality giving a normal whiteness, whereas the body of high quality china gives a brilliant whiteness and greater translucency. The decorations applied

were generally of one colour only, and the standard of transfer printing was often poor. Percy intended to improve all these aspects. In
1893, a particularly poor year for British exports, he visited the
Chicago Exhibition in order to study the characteristics of the
American market. He returned with the view that in order to exploit
the potential there, it was necessary to produce china dinner services
with more elaborate decorations. A number of artists were accordingly
engaged, headed by a man named Micklewright; they painted fish,
game, and landscape subjects on course plates, all of which were
intended for export.

On the home front also, improvements were taking place. In
September 1893 the *Pottery Gazette* wrote about 'the energetic manner in
which the manufactory is now being carried on'. The depression in the
china trade seemed not to have affected the Foley Works: extensions
had been made and more were planned. A policy, which was maintained in later years, was initiated of making a wide range of services:
teasets, breakfast sets, 'five o'clock' teasets with additional pieces to
serve high-tea, 'solitaire' sets for one person, and dessert ware. The
patterns were now described as 'rich and varied, showing that much
thoughtful care has been exercised in their selection, the colours
employed being particularly good'. Table decorations were created in
new shapes and fern pots, vases and flower holders in plain white china
were produced in a variety of styles.

It seems that the products of Wileman & Co. were also to the
public's taste: the sales aspect of the enterprise certainly developed.
London showrooms were set up at the same address as had been used
by J. F. Wileman, and an agent was appointed in Melbourne, Australia.
Describing themselves as 'manufacturers of art porcelain', they had by
1896 appointed a special representative for the U.S.A. and Canada.

At this time Joseph Shelley was suffering with illness: he eventually
died in June 1896. Percy Shelley, now thirty-six, was thus firmly in
control of the business and in this role was to make important
decisions, especially concerning the artists he chose to employ, which
would set the reputation of the company on a firm footing.

The first known of these artists was a man named Rowland Morris.
He had been a pupil of the famous French sculptor, M. Hughues
Protât, who was the modelling master at the Stoke and Hanley Schools
of Art as well as working for Minton's. Following a period working
for one of the firms in the Potteries, Morris gained a place at the
National Art Training School in South Kensington. From there he was

3 Teaware, ribbed shape 1886, blue pattern 1888

to undertake the important work of terracotta panels for the Wedgwood Institute, Burslem, modelled in 1870. These include a series depicting the months of the year, on the façade of the building, and a series illustrating the processes of potting, some carried out in conjunction with Matthew Elden, one-time art director of Minton's Art Pottery Studio at South Kensington. Morris later returned to the pottery firms, designing ornamental china for Bernard Moore at the St Mary's Works (later Thos. C. Wild's), as well as china and the recently developed statuary porcelain, Parian, at St Gregory's Works for J. S. Wilson (later Jackson & Gosling).

The exact years of Rowland Morris's association with Wileman & Co. are not known. Indeed, he may never have been wholly employed by them; it was the practice at that time for artists such as Micklewright, modellers such as Morris, and even decorators, to be employed by a number of firms, either simultaneously or in very quick succession for particular commissions. However, in March 1896 one of Morris's designs was entered with the Design Registry and this shape was to have a considerable effect on the firm in the future.

The Dainty White range with its fluted panels and scallopped edges was produced in a higher quality body than were many of the earlier ranges. At first it was available only in plain white. Some regard the shape as influenced by French designs: this is indeed possible, for besides Morris's earlier connection with Protât, and the general influence at that time of a strong 'foreign contingent' in the potteries, the modeller employed full-time by Wileman & Co. was also French. M. Maxime Avoine, a sculptor who had worked on buildings in London in the 1880s before being offered a position at Minton's in Stoke, was to remain modeller for many years, and he assisted Morris in the task of creating the originals from which moulds were made of the Dainty White range. This could have amounted to about one hundred pieces.

This shape was to be by far the most successful ever produced by Wileman & Co., or indeed Shelley in any of its later forms, and is regarded by many as synonymous with the name of Shelley. Dainty White was the longest-lasting shape, being produced from 1896 to the close-down of the firm in 1966. Indeed, in one sense it outlasted the Shelley enterprise, since it was produced for one year by the take-over firm in order to comply with commitments in the U.S.A., and was later remodelled by that firm though with little success. Besides the plain white version, later alternatives included Floral Dainty with a modelled and painted flower in the handles, and various applied decoration versions, some with transfer printing inside or out, some with overall effects. Dainty White also formed the base for much of the commemorative ware which was made.

In November 1898, Rowland Morris died at Hanley. The journal *Artist* included in its obituary the prophetic comment: 'It is a sad reflection that the name of Rowland Morris has been lately out of mind, and the fact that in recent years he had been employed as a modeller for articles of pottery, with the production of which usually the manufacturer's name is the only one associated, partly accounts for the obscurity in which the work of this clever artist has been enveloped.' Despite *Artist*'s low regard for articles of pottery, the public has shown its appreciation for Rowland Morris's design and it is to be hoped that readers of this book may now associate his name, as well as that of Shelley, with a lasting success.

4 Dainty White teaware, modelled by Rowland Morris, 1896

Evidence of Percy Shelley's ability to select good craftsmen of all types is not based solely on his choice of Rowland Morris. At around the same time he also employed as artistic director a man who was later described in the *Pottery and Glass Record* as 'one of the most talented and versatile ceramic designers of recent times'. This man was Frederick Rhead. Such is the importance of this man that it is worth recording the main aspects of his career at this point, including of course the significant years he spent employed under Percy Shelley.

Frederick was born in Newcastle-under-Lyme in 1857, into a family with many important contributions to pottery and to art. His father, George Woolliscroft Rhead (1832–1908) was well known as an artist and also as an art instructor at Newcastle-under-Lyme School of Art and Fenton Art School. He had been associated with Brown-Westhead & Co., and had been appointed heraldic artist for Minton's. George's father and uncle, Sampson and George Rhead, are known to have operated a pottery in Stoke in the 1840s: their uncle, John Daniel (d. 1821), had managed the famous New Hall Pottery at Shelton for many years, while his father before him, Ralph Daniel, was once reputed to have brought from France to the Potteries the use of plaster of Paris moulds, thus making obsolete the use of brass moulds. Earlier roots of the family in North Staffordshire date back to the sixteenth century.

With such a background it is perhaps not surprising that Frederick became a student at art school and won a number of national medals and Queen's prizes for pottery art. He also became a pupil of the renowned Louis Marc Solon at Minton's. Solon was another of the many continental artists who came to the area, and specifically to Minton's, following the upheaval of the Franco-Prussian war in 1870. His famed speciality was decoration in pâte-sur-pâte, a process whereby the artist used liquid clay instead of colour to paint or 'lay on' his design. Successive layers, each drying before the next, were applied so that the image was built up in relief before its final glaze. The end result of this laborious process was very delicate, generally in white slip on a deep-coloured background, and was probably Minton's best-known contribution to Victorian ceramics. The firm's archives include mention of Frederick Rhead in the pâte-sur-pâte records, listing pieces decorated by him between 1875 and 1877.

It seems surprising by modern standards that an artist should be creating such mature works at such an early age. Frederick was working with Solon by 1872 when only fifteen years old. However, the standards of that time were different from today's: apprenticeships sometimes started at the age of thirteen, and in the pottery industry artists commonly received their art college education in the evenings.

At about the age of twenty, Frederick moved to work for Josiah Wedgwood & Sons in Etruria. This move would seem a little strange, given the excellent reputation of Minton's at that time and the high regard their pâte-sur-pâte artists earned, were it not for the insights given by a Stoke Magistrates' Court report of February 1878. The case reported was that of Frederick Rhead being charged with 'having at divers times feloniously stolen a quantity of coloured clays of the value of 1 shilling, the property of Messrs. Mintons'. The prosecution centred on a particular plate which Frederick (now described as assistant master at Stoke School of Art) had decorated in pâte-sur-pâte while he was a student at that school some years earlier, and which had been sent to the South Kensington Museum, as the work of a pupil, where it had won a prize. Somehow Minton's had become aware of the fact that their own clays were used in the work, and now the leading names of the firm were to give evidence against Frederick: Leon Arnoux, the art director, said that the colours were his speciality and their composition a secret. Rhead replied that he did not know the secret and had done nothing more towards divulging a secret than Minton's did every time they sold a vase. Louis Solon confirmed under cross-examination that he was in the habit of taking colours home. Colin Minton Campbell appeared to confirm that he had not given Rhead permission to take any clays, but as patron of the School of Art was reminded of the rule that students' materials were supplied by manufacturers. For the defence, Mr R. F. Abrahams of Copeland's confirmed the custom of taking clays home, and called the prosecution 'intensely cruel'. After an adjournment, Minton's said they would withdraw the prosecution if Frederick would make certain admissions. Frederick replied that he had never dreamt he had been acting feloniously and he would not for one moment admit that he had done so. Nevertheless the case was withdrawn.

Further investigation reveals that Wedgwood's were at first rather wary of taking Frederick into their employ. The three brothers, Godfrey, Clement and Lawrence, deliberated and communicated with each other (and in the process of their interviews with Frederick gained knowledge of Minton's materials and techniques). Finally he was engaged at £3 per week subject to various conditions, one of which was 'to mix his own colours but to make no secret of the mixings'. Clement's letters also show that Frederick's younger brother Louis (of whom more later) was drawn into the affair, with Minton Campbell wanting to discharge Louis on an unfounded accusation of impudence to M. Arnoux. 'This opens one's eyes to their methods', remarked Clement Wedgwood to Godfrey.

While at Wedgwood's, Frederick appears to have exercised his earlier skills at the same time as developing new ones. At the Universal Exhibition, Paris, in 1878 Wedgwood displayed four pieces of his work, and others decorated to his design. Two were pâte-sur-pâte, a classical design and a not-so-classical Egyptian snake-charmer: the other two were large plaques in sgraffito technique decorated with medieval subjects. The latter two may reflect the influence of Godfrey Wedgwood who supervised the production of 'modern wares' at that time, such as the tiles created by art director Thomas Allen who had also just moved from Minton's. Exactly how long Frederick worked for Wedgwood's is not known. Some time later he designed for E. J. Bodley & Sons at the Hill Pottery, Burslem, a firm which produced high quality china up to about 1890, and in 1885 he is reported as employed at the Burslem firm of Gildea. No records of his production there are known to the present authors.

Yet another move saw Frederick working for the firm of William Brownfield & Sons, of Cobridge. It is unclear when exactly he joined the firm, but probably one of his earliest pieces is the most celebrated. This is the Gladstone Testimonial Vase which was commissioned by members of the Burslem Liberal Club to present to William Gladstone following his third period as Prime Minister. The vase was designed and decorated in *pâte-sur-pâte* by Frederick, and a contemporary description shows the classical leanings of this style of work:

In the centre is a symbolical figure of Liberty: on the right is Homer and on the left Dante offering the poet's tribute. Next to the central figure on the left are figures of a vestal in a pleading attitude and an historian recording the deeds done in the name of freedom. On the back of the vase in the centre is a figure of St. George, supported on one side by William Wallace and on the other by Brian Boru.

Also included are figures of Ireland, Poland and 'saucy children'. Despite the historical licence, it is a striking vase, of classical shape with a narrow foot and neck. It was first displayed at the Wedgwood Institute, Burslem (which had been opened by Gladstone), and was presented to him in August 1888. One report suggests that Frederick Rhead himself handed the vase to the statesman. This fine example is now the property of Sir William Gladstone who has recently allowed it to be put on long-term display at the Gladstone Pottery Museum, Longton.

In 1883 William Brownfield had withdrawn from the firm and in 1892 Arthur Brownfield reconstructed the pottery on a co-operative basis with himself as 'chief worker' and the workmen as shareholders. This Brownfield Guild Pottery originally retained the same art director, Louis Jahn, who had joined them from Minton's in 1872, but when Jahn returned to Minton's after Arnoux's retirement, he was replaced by Frederick Rhead. It seems that this may have been an unhappy period: Frederick wrote of the labour force, 'As workmen, under the old system, they were honest, efficient, and valuable servants; but under the "Guild" their performances were grotesque.' The opinion was later advanced that 'the ideals and work of Mr. Rhead do not seem to have been adequately appreciated by the committee of workmen who managed the Brownfield Guild Pottery'. The proceedings are reported to have become chaotic and around 1898 the Guild was wound up; but by 1896 Frederick had already been producing drawings for Percy Shelley.

Thus, before he moved to Wileman & Co., Frederick Rhead had experienced working with firms who produced a wide range of pottery. More important, he had worked alongside some of the most important designers and artists of the late Victorian period, such as

Solon, Allen, and Jahn. Less directly, he had been influenced by Arnoux and Protât. It is interesting to note also the prominence of the name of Minton in Frederick's career, as indeed it dominated the English and many overseas markets. Even though design throughout this period tended to rely on reviving Renaissance and oriental inspirations, such a grounding for a young artist was undoubtedly very sound – a base for moving on to more original work.

In the first years of his art directorship at Wileman & Co. Frederick did create designs for *pâte-sur-pâte* (including one incorporating a favourite motif of Solon's for the technique – the spider's web), but there is only tenuous evidence that any of these were put into production. Rhead's reputation was to be founded more on a series of effects he used on earthenware. These were given the names Intarsio, Spano-Lustra, Urbato, Primitif and Pastello wares.

At this stage in his career Frederick Rhead was a man with a vision: he wrote of 'sweetening every cupboard in the kingdom with daintier china and healthier looking earthenware'. He enthused about the possibilities for designers to exercise real artistic powers in the creation of articles which were to be mass-produced. In some areas, such as furniture, metalwork, fabrics and wall-papers, where the influence of William Morris, Charles Voysey, Walter Crane and the style of l'Art Nouveau was being felt, Frederick saw signs of progress. But about the pottery industry, 'the very industry which is susceptible of the most varied and the highest artistic treatment', he was scathing in his comments. These were mainly directed towards the revivalist period during which he had been trained and in particular he wrote cynically that 'the result of our supreme efforts has been on view at international exhibitions for thirty years past. Imitations of Old Dresden – replicas of Old Sèvres. Vases covered with wobbling cupids and smirking nymphs, patches of loud colour and gilt scrolls – imitations of bronze, of cast iron, of lace, of ivory, of almost everything that could be imitated; but of porcelain and its own inherent beauty, little or nothing.' Thus it was in a mood of showing that art and commercialism were not necessarily hostile to each other and with a view to creating new designs that Frederick Rhead began to work for Wileman & Co.

Intarsio, which proved to be the most popular and longest-lasting of the effects Rhead introduced, used the technique of applying the painted decoration to the earthenware object before it was glazed. Underglaze decoration of this type resulted in the complete fusion of the colours with the glaze and was seen by some as superior to the effects which enamel colours could give. The range of shades used was quite extensive: deep greens, browns and blues were often used for backgrounds to set off the brilliance which some other colours, especially orange and a particular apple green, achieved in underglaze effect (see colour plate I).

The trade name Intarsio was probably derived from the Italian word *intarsia* which means inlay, or inlaid work (in a variety of possible media). It would not, however, be fair to suggest that this style of work was generated by Italian art: the influences are more likely to be Dutch in origin, together with the impression made on Frederick by some of his contemporaries. Thomas Allen at Wedgwood, for example, was known for his underglaze work and at Minton's W. S. Coleman used the technique to good effect, impressing Frederick and one of his brothers, George, who worked closely with Coleman. The Dutch influence may be traced to two articles which Frederick wrote for the journal *Artist*, extolling the artistic virtues of Rozenburg wares. The underglaze decoration in low-toned colours was described as 'a joy to the student of ceramics' and in Frederick's opinion had no equal amongst British ceramics. It is obvious that he travelled to Holland for these two articles and a third on Delft; a folder of his work contains thumbnail pencil sketches of Dutch scenes, and Dutch characters appeared on some of the later Intarsio ware.

A considerable number of patterns were produced, many of which were applied only to one shape. The decorations were hand-painted by female decorating staff who numbered two hundred at the turn of the century. The company's pattern book provides a record of fifty-six patterns in Intarsio ware, in the form of the outline transfers which were applied before filling in by hand. Illustrations and examples of many other Intarsio patterns are known. Each has a four-digit pattern number, generally transfer-printed on the base. These numbers appear to have started in series at 3000 and the pattern book (which only contains Intarsio patterns which are identifiably Frederick Rhead's) stops at pattern no. 3388. Therefore, if every number was used there could be nearly four hundred designs. Percy Shelley, who had already been making good use of the Patents, Designs and Trade Marks Act of 1883, registered many of the designs, the first group of forty being entered in December 1898.

There are various styles to be found in the Intarsio series. The earlier examples often incorporated bands of a repeating design which

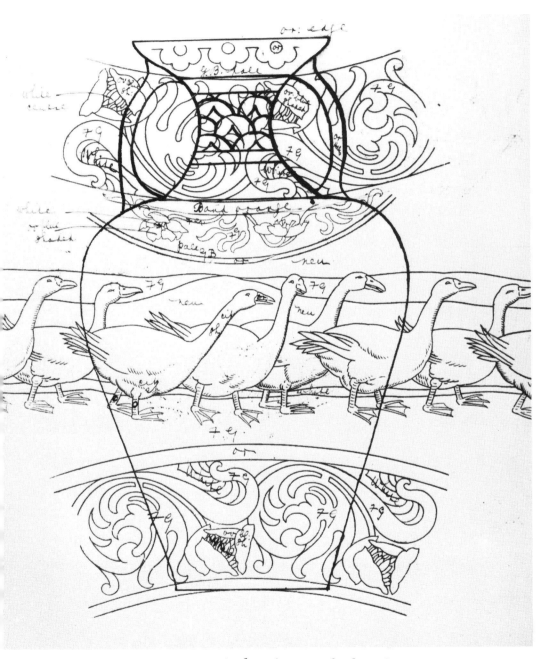

5 Intarsio pattern 3165, from the pattern book, c. 1899

6 Ewers in Intarsio ware, 1898

featured flower motifs in the predominant section. Others showed the
repetition of earlier themes, such as the Egyptian example from
Frederick's time at Wedgwood. Later patterns included bands featuring
a variety of animals: lambs, cats, swans, ducklings, geese, fish and
hens. Some of these may have shown the influence of W. S. Coleman's
work which had impressed Frederick during his apprenticeship at
Minton's. A series introduced in about 1901 used themes and famous
lines from Shakespearean plays to decorate the ware: these (up to

7 Variety of Intarsio pieces, 1899

8 Intarsio ware, Shakespeare style, c. 1900

around pattern no. 3500) were probably the last designs which Frederick Rhead created for Intarsio ware.

The shapes used were also striking: vases with multiple handles; elongated coffee-pots; jugs with sweeping, twisted handles; loving-cups and pilgrim bottles; chalices and flower holders with wide loop handles – these were the basic forms. A series of clock cases was produced with decorated panels depicting various themes related to time: 'Day and Night', 'Polly Put the Kettle On', 'Old Father Time' and 'The

Grim Reaper'. Some also carried relevant mottos in a Victorian style such as 'Wake Up and Get to Business' (see colour plate III).

One particular version of Intarsio which was introduced in about 1900 was a range of character teapots. These featured several politicians including Joseph Chamberlain, Lord Salisbury and, of course, W. E. Gladstone. The body of the pot is the same in each case, although the size differs from a slim version to a more portly one, and the politician's head forms the lid of the pot.

The range of sizes of these earthenware productions was considerable. Small vases of about 10 cm (4 in.) in height were produced alongside the largest items – umbrella stands and jardinières on pedestals – which were over ten times that height (see colour plate II).

The next style to be introduced was Spano-Lustra ware, and this used a completely different style of decoration on earthenware: the sgraffito technique. Also from an Italian word, meaning scratched ware, and originally used as a type of wall decoration, sgraffito involves a process of covering the earthenware piece in one or more layers of various coloured slips and then removing by hand, with a simple, sharp, pointed tool, portions of these layers to create the pattern. Examples of Spano-Lustra ware may, for instance, be made in a deep, reddish earthenware with a white and green slip covering the outside surface. These outer layers are then selectively removed to leave the pattern, and the whole is finally covered in a lustre glaze. Although the name of this series may have been stimulated by the early pottery known as Hispano-Moresque, a name later used by Bernard Moore, the actual designs do not show any strong Spanish or Moorish influence. A number of the patterns include repeating leaf or flower motifs and one celebrated design uses a very bold lobster and wave design.

The third earthenware range, Urbato, used a further development of the sgraffito technique, by using numerous layers of coloured slip instead of the single layer traditionally used, or the one or two in Spano-Lustra ware. This was, therefore, a more complex style, and additional colours were painted on with a brush if desired. A plain glaze completed the process.

Few surviving examples of Urbato ware are known. The designs again often incorporated floral or plant motifs but some abstract patterns were used, as well as a repeating design of penguins! The clock case in colour plate III bears the Urbato backstamp but is decorated in the technique called tube-lining – a similar process to icing fine lines on to a cake.

9 Intarsio character teapot depicting Lord Salisbury, 1900

12 Variety of Urbato ware, 1899

Primitif ware is also rare to find. A description in *Artist*, 1899, states:

In this the effects are obtained (as is the case in the finest antique Japanese and Chinese pottery) by what may be described as 'directed accident'. The effects are all accidental, but are always more or less under the control of the artist, who knows with tolerable accuracy what the general effect will be, but who never knows exactly what delightful passages of colour may gather in certain parts or what beautiful play of textures and lines, like the swirl of water round and over stepping-stones in a brook.

The last named range is Pastello, which consists of 'figures, flowers, and various natural objects executed on a dark ground, cameo-fashion, in a semi-transparent paste'. This description might well be that of a *pâte-sur-pâte* technique: it is known that Frederick Rhead did not like the attribution of this effect to the French (because of its title) and so perhaps he chose the Italian-sounding name. Again, no examples are known to have survived, but as the popularity of this ware was short-lived it is possible that only a few items of this line were produced. The previously mentioned designs in *pâte-sur-pâte* for Wileman & Co. give an indication of what might have been part of the Pastello series.

Of the five named series, Intarsio was by far the most popular, judging both by references to it in trade journals and by the number of pieces which still survive. Indeed, the output of the earthenware ranges must have been considerable, for extra land was bought in 1891 and the works were continually enlarged, first to incorporate larger china works and later to include the new earthenware factory along with offices, showrooms and warehouses, all in the three-storey style.

10 *opposite top*: Two vases showing the sgraffito technique: left, Spano-Lustra; right, Urbato, *c.* 1900

11 *opposite*: Jug with Urbato decoration, 1898

13 Design for a vase, possibly Pastello ware, by Frederick Rhead, 1897

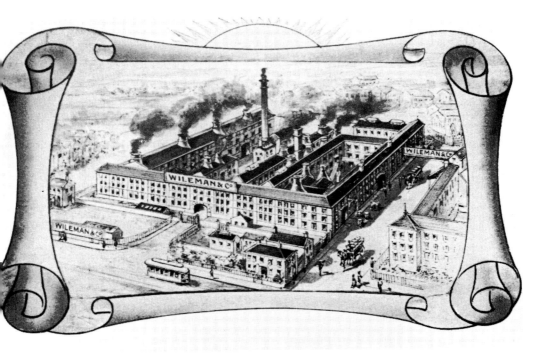

14 Wileman & Co. factory view, c. 1900

By 1898, therefore, the combined china and earthenware works had taken up the basic layout they were to maintain. There were now a number of inner quadrangles, extra ovens and additional one-storey buildings which were used for storage. It is also significant that Wileman & Co. began to refer to their works as the Foley Potteries, a title which J. F. Wileman's neighbouring works had given up only a few years earlier.

The above-named series of earthenware were not the only innovations from Frederick Rhead. Very popular in the late Victorian period was a style of ornaments which were termed 'grotesques'. These were small pieces deliberately made to look ugly or disturbing and they were most often based on animal or semi-human forms. Some potteries, such as Bretby, specialized strongly in this type of production and no doubt made some of their living by gracing many drawing-rooms with graceless objects. Frederick's examples generally had a slightly less than grotesque quality and seemed to represent fantastic or mythical animals. The origin of the grotesque fashion is said to belong to

15 Design for a grotesque by Frederick Rhead, 1899

Japanese ivory carving, and certainly oriental dragons and lions formed part of the range.

Other earthenware, which did not adhere to any of the particular decorative styles so far listed, was also being produced, often carrying the Wileman & Co. backstamp and the label 'Faïence'. Wall plates, vases and other objects are known, some of which bear the names of the individual artists employed at the time, such as Stephen Hartley, R. Seadon, Messrs Banks, Wood and Forester, and the Misses Robinson, Price and Brown. It is further recorded in *Artist*, 1899, that other artists, such as P. G. Riley and a Mrs Waterhouse, had supplied designs just before the turn of the century.

The response to Wileman & Co.'s products seems to have been an enthusiastic one. In 1899 an article in the journal *Artist*, entitled 'Some Beautiful English Pottery', was devoted completely to what was then being termed Foley Art Pottery. It was reported that Wileman's 'had the courage to fling aside all the cherished traditions of the modern British potter, and have been rewarded by the instant approval of the buying public'. One of the main setters of fashion at that time, Liberty's of Regent Street in London, exhibited a selection of the wares in the same year.

16 Grotesques and jugs, 1899

Notwithstanding the considerable activity in earthenware production, and the success of Percy Shelley's decision to embark upon it, Frederick was also creating designs for china and other media. Elegant, finely executed patterns for dinner- and teaware, and elaborate yet stylish decorations for toilet sets were produced at this time, not to mention another form of sgraffito ware, this time in glazed Parian (the statuary porcelain developed by Minton and Spode).

On reflection, the sheer quantity of new designs, shapes and styles which Frederick Rhead created for Wileman & Co. makes it the more surprising that he only worked for the company for about nine years. By 1905 his position had been taken over by the next art director, Walter Slater, and Frederick had moved on yet again. Perhaps his high output reflected the freedom afforded him by Percy Shelley to take risks with the designs which were marketed. Certainly Frederick's career flourished in his forties for he began to expand his artistic and intellectual talents. While at Wileman's he wrote a number of articles on pottery decoration and joined with two of his brothers in illustrating a number of books, among them John Bunyan's *Pilgrim's Progress* and Defoe's *Robinson Crusoe*.

Frederick's brothers are worthy of mention, not only because 'the

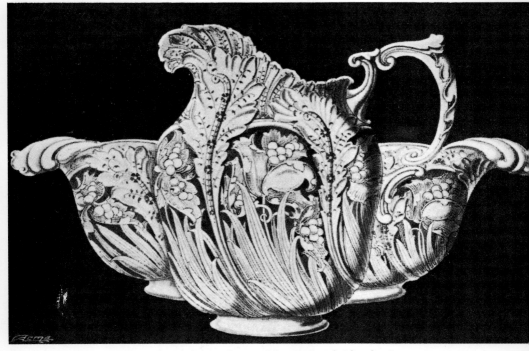

17 Toilet set designed by Frederick Rhead, 1897

18 Sgraffito ware in glazed Parian by Frederick Rhead, c. 1900

19 Later designs by Frederick Rhead, c. 1902

three Messrs. Rhead' are credited with designing for Percy Shelley, but also because they exemplify the extraordinary calibre of the Rhead family. George Woolliscroft Rhead junior (1855–1920) was the eldest. He trained at Minton's with W. S. Coleman at the South Kensington Art Pottery Studio and later turned to painting, with the result that he exhibited at the Royal Academy for over forty years. He executed stained glass, frescoes and murals for buildings in London, Manchester and Chichester, but was most noted for his etchings and illustrations (he designed the cover for Liberty's Christmas catalogue in 1893). In 1896 George became design master at Putney School of Art, then director of the Southwark Polytechnic Institute, and he published many books on design, ceramics and other decorative arts (including a monumental work, The History of the Fan, which led to his designing Queen Mary's coronation fan).

One of Frederick and George's most notable joint efforts was their 1906 book Staffordshire Pots and Potters (recently reprinted in facsimile:

20 Illustration by Frederick Rhead from *Pilgrim's Progress*, 1898

LIBERTY

YULE TIDE

GIFTS
FOR
1893

LONDON   & PARIS

21 Liberty's Christmas catalogue cover by George Woolliscroft Rhead, 1893

see bibliography). This book obviously relies on the personal experience of the two brothers at various potteries, and the accumulated experience of the family. Well illustrated, including many of their own line drawings, and written in a lively style, this work demonstrates their love for the subject matter.

The third brother, Louis (1858–1927), started his art training in Paris at the tender age of thirteen. After also training in London, he worked for some time in the pottery industry. This included a period at Minton's which was terminated when Frederick moved to Wedgwood: Louis joined him there, and the following year he exhibited a plaque at the Paris Exhibition of 1878. He continued this work on an irregular basis up to 1882 while he was studying art in London and living in Chelsea, and then accepted a full-time position again. After just a year, however, he moved to the U.S.A. to become art manager for the publishers Appleton's. In America he developed various aspects of his artistry, including the design of posters in the style of l'Art Nouveau with exhibitions in New York, London and Paris; oils and watercolours; illustrations for magazines such as Harper's Bazaar; and tooled leather book-covers. From 1911–27 he focused on book illustration, publishing for Harper's a series of popular classics until the year of his death.

For Frederick also, later life was a time of development and change. After leaving Wileman & Co. he is known to have been producing designs for fire-screens and fancy-dress, writing two novels and two comic operas, at the same time as reporting and illustrating for a local newspaper. As far as potting is concerned, Frederick is next heard of working for the firm of Birks, Rawlins & Co. – he was related to the Birks family, members of which had trained with him under Solon. At the Turin Exhibition of 1911 and the Ghent Exhibition of 1913, vases and plaques in pâte-sur-pâte by Frederick attracted attention – some even made use of coloured clays similar to those which had led to his court case in 1878. From 1913–29 he was art director of Wood & Sons, Burslem, including the Crown Pottery which made Bursley ware. During this period Frederick continued writing on pottery themes, including a series of thirteen articles on tiles, but he was also a founder-member and long-time president of the Pottery Managers' and Officials' Association (in which context he was referred to by the Pottery Gazette in 1923 as 'doyen of the art directors of the potteries'). His last position was in charge of the art departments of both Cauldon Potteries of Shelton and the Worcester Royal Porcelain Company.

---

22 Poster by Louis Rhead, 1896

23 Frederick Rhead photographed in 1922

When Frederick died in 1933, the trade magazine *Pottery and Glass Record* described him as 'the Leonardo da Vinci of North Staffordshire'. The *Pottery Gazette and Glass Trade Review* was a little less extreme, noting that he was 'everywhere adjudged to be one of the most talented and versatile ceramic designers of recent times'.

Frederick's contribution to the pottery industry was continued by his children. His daughter, Charlotte, trained with him at Wood's before moving to A. G. Richardson, manufacturers of Crown Ducal, at Cobridge. She later returned to Wood's taking over the art directorship after Frederick had left, which she held until her death in 1947, and producing her own distinctive and collectable designs in Bursley ware. One or two rare examples of her work also bear the mark of Cauldon Potteries.

The eldest son, Frederick Hurten Rhead (1880–1942), no doubt named after C. F. Hürten, a noted artist for Copeland's who had defended Frederick in his 1878 trial, became art director to Thomas Forester & Son of Longton before moving to the U.S.A. in 1902. There he made his mark on a number of potteries, while his younger brother, Harry G. Rhead, also in America, became art director for the American Mosaic Tile Company.

The years Frederick Rhead was employed at Wileman & Co. were important ones in the development of the company, but the twentieth century was to bring further development and many significant changes as the following chapters will reveal.

4

Into the twentieth century

At the turn of the century, Percy Shelley was in sole charge of the company. His father had died in 1896, and during his thirties Percy had been the driving force behind the growth of the Foley Works. Now, in his forties, he was to steer the company through another difficult period yet at the same time manage further development. He undertook this as the sole representative of the family: none of his children was old enough to contribute – a daughter had died in infancy, his oldest son was only six and the twin sons were five years old.

One of the major problems affecting British industry at this time was that of holding its own in world trade and in the home markets. The dominating position which had been achieved in the late Victorian period was now being threatened by very strong competition from countries such as Germany and the U.S.A. who had taken the lead in some areas. Thus the great debate of the period, and for many years to come, centred on the value of protecting British trade by tariffs or taxes imposed on goods from other countries. Free trade and protectionism were the two opposing factions.

Percy Shelley was a man of strong convictions, but unlike his father, who had been a preacher for the primitive Methodist New Connexion, Percy chose the political rather than religious sphere to make his presence felt. He soon came to be known as a staunch supporter of free trade and an ardent Liberal. In a way he was typical of the Liberal supporters of that period: generally manufacturers and non-conformists, coming from the towns, they represented the demands of industry and sought freedom from artificial restrictions on enterprise. At the same time, many free-traders adopted the attitude (inconsistent by previous standards of *laissez-faire* thinking) that State intervention was necessary in some areas, for example factory and housing conditions, and in this way Percy also became known as a campaigner for better conditions in the pottery industry and a supporter of the growth of trade unionism.

His belief in free trade meant that Percy made rather unpopular suggestions from time to time. In 1905, following a visit to Germany where he had been impressed by some of the techniques in use there, he suggested engaging 'a small band of German workers to open up a small experimental pottery in Longton'. The pottery journals were scathing: the *Pottery Gazette* remarked that 'it would show more enterprise if a promising employee was sent to Germany'.

The 1906 general election saw the Liberals come to power with Percy campaigning hard in his constituency. In a by-election the following year, Percy was therefore a popular choice for the Liberal candidate, but as 'his business could ill spare him' another contender was chosen. Percy may have received some consolation from the fact that he was returned unopposed as councillor for Longton that year.

Working conditions in the pottery industry were in much need of improvement. Numbers of workers contracted industrial illnesses of various sorts, including lead poisoning from the use of some glazes, and lung diseases from the dust created in some parts of the production process. Percy was active in the Joint Committee of manufacturers in achieving new compensation acts and factory controls. Despite these improvements the level and balance of trade was not good: the slump of 1902–4 which followed the Boer War was itself followed by a deeper depression in 1908–9. The buying power of wages dropped, industrial unrest was common and Britain learned again that the greatest industrial disease was unemployment: at that time 8% of trade unionists were out of work. This figure underestimates the seriousness of the situation, since working hours had also been reduced in an attempt to spread more widely the available work.

This severe economic situation had the effect of reducing the number of women in employment: the less scrupulous employers had attempted to employ women as cheap labour to displace men, but the trade unions were effectively campaigning against this trend. In 1910 Percy Shelley was the subject of a rumour that he employed a woman dipper at 12s. 6d. (62½p) per week to displace a man earning two guineas per week. The Mayor of Burslem (secretary of the Ovenmen's Union) investigated and reported that no women dippers were employed, no men were displaced, and in fact the men dippers earned £3 per week.

So it can be seen that in the years leading up to the 1914–18 war there were many difficulties in running a company like Wileman & Co., yet Percy Shelley managed this alongside his public activities. In 1908 he had been elected a magistrate for the county of Stafford and in 1911 for the new federation of towns, Stoke-on-Trent, and he was always active in the North Staffordshire Chamber of Commerce.

In this way one may build up a picture of the man who in essence 'made' Shelley Potteries, a man in many ways typical of the family businessman at the time: strong-willed, a campaigner, and sometimes a hard master over working hours and money matters – a self-made man. Yet at the same time he was representative of the staunch Liberal of the period, with a more human side demonstrating concern for others and enjoyment of life's pleasures (especially dancing!).

Considering the amount of energy Percy Shelley invested in the business, it is possibly surprising that he was slow in associating the family name with the successes of the firm. By 1910 the firm was still titled Wileman & Co. even though James Wileman had left in 1884, and the china produced was still marked Foley China. It was an unintended result of trying to register that as a trade name which eventually led to the name of Shelley China being originated.

The name Foley, as has been mentioned, refers to the area where the works were situated, and is taken from a family of landowners. Of the numerous potteries there, a number have used the name in marking their ware at various times. Possibly the first was J. K. Knight, predecessor of Henry Wileman at the Foley Potteries, who sometimes included the name in his marks from 1846–53. But more important was a pottery just across the road from Wileman's, originally called Robinson & Son. This firm had often included the name Foley China in its marks from 1881, and when it was taken over in 1903, the new owners E. Brain & Co. used the name in all of their marks. Brain's and Wileman's were therefore using the same name to label their china and in the early years of this century their wares increasingly competed with each other. When in 1910 Percy Shelley attempted to register Foley China as the trade name for Wileman & Co., it was Brain's who objected. The conflict culminated in a court case in London, where it was judged that Wileman's could make no exclusive claim to use the name. As a result E. Brain & Co. (who later acquired Coalport China and became part of the Wedgwood Group) continued to use the name Foley in their back-stamp, as did some of their neighbours (James Kent and J. Goodwin-Stoddard & Co.) in later years. But Percy Shelley now needed a new mark.

Consequently, in 1910 the now familiar Shelley mark was originated with the family name enclosed in the outline shield shape. For a few years the phrase Late Foley was incorporated and in Shelley advertising the public was notified of the change-over in strong terms – one statement read: 'The world-wide reputation of "Foley" China has caused many cheap imitations and in future, to protect the public, the real and genuine "Foley" China will always be indelibly marked "Shelley" China, a trademark which is a guarantee of the highest excellence.'

It was in this way that twentieth-century Shelley wares originated; but in order to appreciate those wares to the full it is necessary to introduce the man who took over as art director from Frederick Rhead – Walter Slater.

Walter Slater's background in ceramic art was as impressive as that of the Rhead family. His great-grandfather, William (c. 1784–1864) was the decorative manager at the Nottingham Road Works in Derby during one of its most famous periods, but on the closure of the works in 1848 he moved to Davenport's near Burslem. William's two sons had been apprentices at Derby: the elder, William (c. 1807–65), became designer and manager at Davenport's for over thirty years, while the younger, Joseph (1812–96), went to the Hill Pottery, Burslem, under Samuel Alcock – the same works where Frederick Rhead designed for E. J. Bodley & Sons thirty years later. Joseph Slater then made an important move to Minton's and after approximately ten years working for that firm moved to Brown-Westhead & Moore in Burslem, a successor to Ridgway's. (It was this same firm for which G. W. Rhead senior had worked earlier, and which later became the Cauldon Pottery where Frederick Rhead was employed.)

Joseph's move to Minton's was important because it meant that all four of his sons could start their training in ceramic art at one of the foremost potteries of the time. The eldest son, William (the third), had been one of the last apprentices at Derby and had moved with his father to the Hill Pottery where, under the control of Sir James Duke and Nephews, he produced the elaborately painted level used by Gladstone when laying the foundation stone of the Wedgwood Institute in 1863. After a few years at Minton's he became art director to Harvey Adams & Co. – the same Harvey Adams who had been a partner with

J. B. Shelley at the Dresden Works. The second son, George, is known to have worked at Minton's in the 1880s before embarking on a lengthy career as an artist for Doulton's. The third son, Albert, started as a flower painter for Minton's but then moved to manage the firm of Pinder, Bourne & Co. for eight years before designing for the noted tile firm of Minton, Hollins & Co. for more than thirty years. Finally, the youngest son, John (1844–1916), moved from Minton's to Pinder, Bourne & Co. after Albert had left but shortly before that firm was taken over by Doulton's in their first expansion from London to the Potteries in 1877. He remained designer and art manager for nearly forty years, introduced a number of styles of decoration for which Doulton's are now famous, and was instrumental in initiating the production of bone china at Burslem. He patented chiné ware, achieved by impressing lace or fabric on to wet clay; a photographic process to transfer designs on to pottery; and a metallic pipe joint for sanitary fittings which enabled the ceramic pipe to be soldered to metal.

With such a family background it is perhaps not surprising that when Albert, the third of the brothers mentioned above, had two sons both of them made their careers in the pottery industry. The younger, Frederick Slater, became a modeller for the Irish pottery of Belleek, but it is the elder, Walter Slater, who is of particular interest here. Born in about 1865, Walter followed the example of his father and uncles by becoming an apprentice at Minton's. This would have been during the late 1870s, about the same time as the Rheads were leaving the firm. Sadly, the Minton archives contain no reference to the work carried out by Walter Slater, nor is it known under which of the artists he trained. However, by about 1885 Walter had moved to work for Doulton's at the works they had recently taken over in Nile Street, Burslem, under the direction of his uncle, John Slater.

Walter Slater worked for twenty years at Doulton's: for the first half of that period the examples of his work which survive show that he was an artist of merit, especially with floral subjects. Dessert plates featuring ledges painted with pansies and a gold floral border; other plates with yellow and pink roses: these, either signed or bearing the artist's monogram, are the style of the time. For the 1893 Chicago Exhibition, which marked the peak of Henry Doulton's career and coincided with Percy Shelley's interest in decorated ware, Walter's contribution included dinnerware with elaborate decoration. A cover-dish with rococo panels in pale blue, painted with English garden flowers and with roses between the panels, is now in the Sydney Museum of Applied Arts and Sciences.

24 Lactolian ware vase by Walter Slater for Doulton, c. 1902

During the latter part of his stay at Doulton's, Walter Slater is known to have worked on the more modern wares which might now be termed Art Nouveau. Lactolian ware, for example, included bone china vases with decorations giving a milky effect. By 1900 these were described as challenging the position of Sèvres china in the market and at exhibitions. Walter also lent his talent to some of the effects which had earlier been created by his uncle, John. Among these was Spanish ware, a form of decoration, mainly on vases and often in deep blue, which used raised gold outline for floral and other subjects. Examples still survive, either signed or monogrammed by Walter Slater. It is also recorded that Walter produced examples of Hyperion and Luscian ware, a form of on-glaze decoration. Charles Noke, who had come to Burslem at John Slater's request and was to become one of Doulton's most famous art directors, described Walter's work as of 'highest quality'.

By 1905, therefore, Walter had gathered much experience with the Doulton factory, and it seems likely that Percy Shelley would have been aware of Walter's work and would certainly have known of the Slater family. It is not known why Frederick Rhead left the position of art director at Wileman's, or how Walter Slater was appointed, but the close contact between pottery firms and families would no doubt have been enough for Percy Shelley to see in Walter a man capable of carrying on the production of increasingly high quality wares.

However, the time at which he joined the Foley Works was not a particularly hopeful one for artistic experiment. The economic depression of the first decade of the century has already been mentioned, together with its devastating effects on British industry at that time. Although the firm was thriving in comparison with some others in the area, it was still a relatively small business whose ability to take risks was still very dependent on a healthy basic trade.

This, then, was the time for a pottery to ensure its financial security, and the particular way which Shelleys chose was to diversify their production to include wares which had previously not been attempted. The Edwardian home was not acquiring new china services and earthenware art pottery, so Walter Slater found himself at first supervising the design of more popular wares: toilet sets; children's ware; domestic earthenware such as jelly moulds; and souvenir china with views, and heraldic and commemorative designs (described in chapter 5).

Nevertheless, by the time the economic situation had improved, Walter was given more artistic freedom. In 1911 a new series of

I Intarsio ware designed by Frederick Rhead, 1897–9

FOR
OUR
CUSTOMERS
USE

THE FOLEYCHINA

DEPÔT
for
THE FOLEY CHINA
ENGLAND'S
FINEST PORCELAIN

II Umbrella stands with Intarsio decoration, and an advertising tile, *c.* 1900

III Clock cases with Intarsio and Urbato decorations, c. 1897–1900

IV Intarsio ware, second series, by Walter Slater, 1911–15

V Various lustre wares by Walter Slater, c. 1919–21

VI The Shelley Girl advertising figure, c. 1925

VII (a) *opposite top*: Queen Anne shape coffee sets in Archway of Roses and Blue Iris patterns, 1928 and 1927

VII (b) *opposite*: Queen Anne shape teaware in various patterns, 1927–9

VIII (a) Nursery teaset by Mabel Lucie Attwell, 1926
VIII (b) Nursery teaset by Hilda Cowham, 1928

25 Intarsio ware, second series, by Walter Slater, 1911

Intarsio ware was introduced. This used the same technique of under-glaze decoration on earthenware as had been used fifteen years previously, but the designs were new and reflected the contemporary style. The patterns (described by one trade reviewer as 'inherently capricious' and 'essentially assertive without bordering on the blatant') were free-flowing abstract forms in what might nowadays be termed an Art Nouveau style. The colours used included some of the deep shades of the original series, but now some brighter tones were also incorporated in harmony. Yellows, pinks and one particularly bright green contributed to an effect which is reminiscent of a Persian style. As far as shapes were concerned, some from the earlier series were retained but the more elaborate forms did not survive. New, relatively straightforward shapes were added: some attracted the description 'exceedingly quaint, in fact almost audacious, though alluring nevertheless' (see colour plate IV).

Pieces produced included numerous vases, jardinières, covered caddies, clock sets and bowls. No evidence is available as to whether the large objects, such as umbrella stands and jardinières with stands, were produced in the second series of Intarsio. Judging by the number of examples which survive, this second series was produced in smaller numbers than the first series. Perhaps the number of years of manufacture was limited by the approaching 1914–18 war: references to Intarsio ware in the trade journals last only as late as 1913.

Other series of ornamental pottery which graced the Edwardian mantelshelf included Flamboyant ware, Surrey Scenery, and the Moon-

26 Toilet sets, c. 1915

light series. The first, as the name may suggest, was the result of Walter Slater's experimentation with flambé glazes. This style of decoration, which had been executed by the ancient Chinese potters, was being revived by a number of potteries, especially Doulton's and Bernard Moore. Requiring a particularly high-temperature firing, the Shelley effects used a deep, brilliant red glaze to achieve flame-like results· Surrey Scenery was a very different style: countryside views illustrating a range of supposedly Surrey subjects were created in the style of Birkett Foster. Printed in black on a gold background, this decoration was applied to the full series of small vases. No examples of the Moonlight series have yet been found.

A further style of decorated earthenware produced at this time was known as Cloisello ware. This featured an underglaze-blue Grecian border with a Chinese daisy in white relief on a blue, patterned background. Despite the mixture of cultural origins, the design was an effective one and no doubt appealed to the public taste at the time. Considering Shelleys' penchant for creating range names which suggest their decorative technique, Cloisello could have been intended as a cloisonné style, but better likenesses of this ancient Chinese technique were in fact produced later (see chapter 5). In the Cloisello range various sizes of jugs are known to have been made, and the pattern was also used for some commemorative items described later.

A particular feature of the early part of the century was the considerable growth of housing in urban areas where the water supply was piped in – but only downstairs. Consequently, earthenware manufacturers found a large market for toilet sets – jug and basin – or toilet services including soap-dish, covered dish and small bowl. Wileman & Co. had produced examples of toilet sets from the beginning of their earthenware production, but Walter Slater created designs which met with increased success. His basic policy seemed to be to use simple styles, and although the names of some of the shapes suggest elaboration – Etruscan, Chippendale, Alexandra – the shapes themselves moved away from earlier complexities and gave a neat, clean line to the pottery. The patterns applied had a similar effect. One in particular featured an all-over ebony black background with a small elegant leaf motif in silver and white – quite a departure from rococo and rosebuds.

As well as the ornamental pottery and earthenware Walter Slater also supervised the development of fine china. The quality of bone china had increased considerably, to the point that in 1910 Mappin & Webb chose Wileman & Co. to manufacture the bone china inserts to their

silver coffee-cup holders. Indeed, Percy Shelley took a keen interest in
the quality and preparation of the raw materials. The bone, which was
imported from South America, where it was a by-product of corned
beef production, was now ground specially for him at the Central Mill,
Hanley, which Percy had founded and to which he sent his staff.

The patterns which Walter Slater created for china at this time again
demonstrated the Eastern influence on his work. The Ashbourne pattern, which was introduced in 1913, was suggestive of a true Japanese
style with colours of red, blue and gold. This pattern was surprisingly
effective when applied to a traditional English shape – Gainsborough –
and in fact it was still being used in 1935. Indeed, up to 1910–19 it
had been the traditional English styles which were the main focus:
plates decorated with scenes from Shakespeare or with fishing scenes
were still well received. However, Walter continued working with
oriental-influenced effects and achieved impressive results.

One development which did not fit this trend was the introduction
of a new shape for teaware in bone china. No doubt stimulated by the
success of the Dainty White shape, Oleander, launched in 1912, was a

27 Ashbourne pattern on china, 1913

fluted shape with no added patterns. The fluting, however, was not an abstract design: the pattern in the body of each piece was in the shape of a leaf or leaves cleverly overlapping to form the shape of the piece. The particular leaf was supposed to be that of the oleander plant and the overall effect in plain white bone china was very delicate.

A final feature of the pre-1914–18 war period which is worthy of mention is the success of Shelleys' china dinner services, especially in the American market. Dinnerware in china, as opposed to high quality earthenware, had always been regarded as a luxury product: in later years Shelleys were to create a strong reputation for this line of product in the U.S.A., and it is important to note that they had made quite a name for themselves as early as 1914.

Shortly before the war two of Percy's sons came to join the family enterprise. The eldest of the three, Percy Norman, was now nineteen years of age and with Vincent Bob (one of the twins), now eighteen, had recently passed the pottery exams of the Stoke-on-Trent Education Committee. The other twin, Kenneth Jack, had at about the same time entered Birmingham University to study for a bachelor's degree in

28 Bowl and vases with Roself and Violette decorations, 1915–16

commerce. In terms of education, Jack (each son was known by his middle name) was following most closely in his father's footsteps, and was arguably to have the most effect in the years following the war.

The 1914–18 war itself had a strong effect on the company. Norman and Bob had to join up while Jack could remain at university. Bob became a captain in his regiment while in France and was a prisoner-of-war for a short while. Meanwhile, in Britain, the trade journals devoted an increasing number of pages to the names of those who would never return from the trenches to work again in the Staffordshire potteries.

At the Foley Works the artistic value of the ware produced presented an almost equally gloomy picture. Of the three new ranges introduced during the war years, it seems more than coincidence that two featured predominantly black backgrounds. Of course, domestic china was not at the forefront of everyone's minds and prices were rising very steeply, so a less expensive mode of decoration was called for.

Roself was introduced in 1915 and took its name from the rose motif originally employed on a self-coloured background. The decorative technique was inexpensive since the basic shape of the rose motif was obtained by a stencil, and the amount of tinting was minimal. A large range of ornamental pottery was available in this effect and although the most common examples bear the black background, others were available such as green, blue, grey, pink, mauve and brown. The obvious success of this line generated the introduction of similar effects but with different flower motifs: violet in 1916 and carnation in 1917. Another effect using mainly black was limited to the smaller range of vases and consisted of a variety of birds hand-painted in bold style and bright colours: the parrot, kingfisher and bluebird were used.

The last wartime series used an effect called Moiré Antique. The name comes from the French word moiré meaning a watered silk, that is, silk which has been treated to give a wavy, damask-like finish. Shelleys' version, on both earthenware and china, was created by applying a print made up of thousands of small vertical lines. The pattern of breaks in this vertical flow created the wavy effect. Pink, blue and green varieties were produced from 1914.

5

Post-war developments

In the year or two following the close of the First World War a number of factors combined to put Wileman & Co. in a particularly strong position for growth and development. All three of Percy's sons were now back with the firm and their different talents and qualities complemented each other well for the task of running a pottery. Norman became more and more concerned with production; Bob, whose flair was for organization, took over the warehouses and stock control; while Jack, with his accountancy training, took charge of the finances. This was the sort of strength that a family business could offer in ideal circumstances.

A second factor was that Walter Slater's son, Eric, had come to join the firm and was working alongside his father. Born in 1902, Eric had originally intended to be an engineer. He had worked for about nine months on the shop-floor of the North Staffordshire Railway Company and for a year in the drawing-office, but he seemed to be getting no nearer his goal. In 1919 he joined the pottery and at the same time started his art training at the local art schools, Stoke for modelling and design, Burslem for design and Hanley for life classes and design – a total of five nights and two afternoons per week. At that time a new Superintendent of Art Instruction had been appointed for these schools: Gordon Forsyth had been an art director, was greatly concerned to improve the level of design in the industry and had a strong influence on the new generation of designers. In all, Eric's training lasted seven years and he won the prize for the best student of the year in 1923.

A third factor was that, contrary to expectation, the armistice was followed by a trade boom which lasted for two years. Wages and prices continued to rise steeply until 1920, when the index of prices stood at three times the level of five years earlier. This peak was not maintained, however, and for some time there was a considerable appreciation of real wages.

A number of effects can be seen to have followed on from this advantageous situation. Money was put into developing the works, and in 1920 an extension in the form of a new office block and showroom was completed. This occupied a space in the area between the existing factory and the main road.

Also at this time, the increased number of persons available for employment meant that the company could develop activities which it had not undertaken previously; for example, promoting its wares by exhibiting at trade fairs. The British Industries Fair of 1920 at Crystal Palace saw a modest stand displaying Shelley China with the three brothers in attendance. This appears to have been the first entry of Wileman & Co. into exhibiting and coincided with a general increase in the number of potteries represented that year. 1920 also saw just a few pieces of Shelley ware at the British Industrial Art Exhibition in Knightsbridge, one of the earliest events staged by the British Institute of Industrial

29 Factory view (from 1950) showing the office block built in 1920

Art. It would seem that these ventures were a success, for the following year at White City the Wileman stand at the British Industries Fair was described as 'one of the best arranged and furnished' and 'one of the most spacious, presenting an exhibit that was full of appealing lines'. The style of display was simple: various tables, shelf units and glass cases were arranged around the allocated area, but someone obviously had an eye for impact – the wall and tables were grey while the curtains and coverings were purple.

However, Shelleys' first association with exhibitions was as short-lived as the economic boom. After two successful years they did not appear at the British Industries Fair again until 1933 when their impact was arguably greater, but of a very different style.

A further opportunity gave Percy Shelley the chance to express his love of reform, again probably made more possible by the presence of others to take responsibility at the works. This was the creation of the Whitley Councils, a series of councils set up on a permanent basis with elected representatives of workers and employers, meeting to consider the well-being of all those connected with the industry. In the post-war scheme for the reconstruction of industry, the Whitley Councils were felt to be vital: they offered hope of reducing the feeling of distance which had grown between employers and the employed, which had contributed to industrial unrest before the war. The pottery industry was chosen to see if the idea was workable and a series of preliminary meetings was set up in 1917. Percy Shelley was in at the start and when the National Council of the Pottery Industry was inaugurated he became a council member. This was obviously a cause that Percy could support wholeheartedly and he gained a reputation for being a 'kindly, considerate and generous personality' during almost twenty years on the council. This involvement included over eighty meetings of the council itself and also the chairmanship of the Research Committee for a number of years. By coincidence one of his fellows on the council for about six years was Frederick Rhead, now in his role as president of the Pottery Managers' and Officials' Association.

At a more local level, Percy's 'public works' also received greater recognition. He became a vice-president of the North Staffordshire Chamber of Commerce during the 1920s, and for many years he was elected president of the North Staffordshire Liberal Federation. But probably the greatest local honour for him was to be nominated for High Sheriff of Staffordshire: this suggestion came during a period of ill-health, however, and was never realized.

The optimistic atmosphere at Wileman & Co., and in the country at large, may help to explain why a particular line of pottery was specially successful at this time. Arms china or heraldic china, together with souvenir china of other types, enjoyed considerable popularity during the very early 1920s, although it disappeared from view in the darker days of the depression to come. Probably a feeling of patriotism after the war, a sense of pride in the community, combined with a greater emphasis on travel around the country, led hundreds of towns to want mementos and souvenirs for residents and visitors. Emblazoned with a coat-of-arms, a vast range of ornaments was produced, often with a slightly jingoistic flavour. Shelleys, too, contributed to this style of pottery.

By 1922 Wileman & Co. had produced over four hundred different shapes of miniature objects: their heraldic catalogue for that year illustrated over two hundred from a series which was numbered 1 to 507 (although some of the later numbers were not used). The exact date when the series started is not known, but examples are known bearing the Wileman & Co. backstamp thus pre-dating the change-over to the Shelley mark in 1910. Early shapes include the usual miniature versions of household wares – jugs, vases, teapots – and of everyday clothing – a boot, clog, top hat, handbag and bishop's mitre. A group of animals includes a grinning camel and a doleful elephant, while a later trio of objects can only be miniature bedpans! A number of the later productions were reduced examples of standard Shelley shapes in vases, coffee-pots and so on, including at least six shapes from the first Intarsio series. Although a small number of miniature buildings and monuments appear, these do not seem to be the outcome of such faithful research and accuracy as those produced by W. H. Goss, for example.

The effect of the 1914–18 war can be seen reflected in the production of miniature aeroplanes, battleships, cannons, ambulances and field guns, together with a miniature fire-place scene labelled 'Keep the Home Fires Burning'. In the years immediately following the war the change of atmosphere is symbolized by the introduction of cigarette cases, miniature open charabancs, motor boats, garden rollers, liners and open four-seater cars.

The china body used in these ornaments was of the high quality in use at the works and all the coats-of-arms were engraved on the site. Hundreds of towns from Aberdeen and Andover to Wallasey and Woolwich submitted orders and were supplied (in 1922 prices) at

30 Heraldic china from a catalogue, 1922

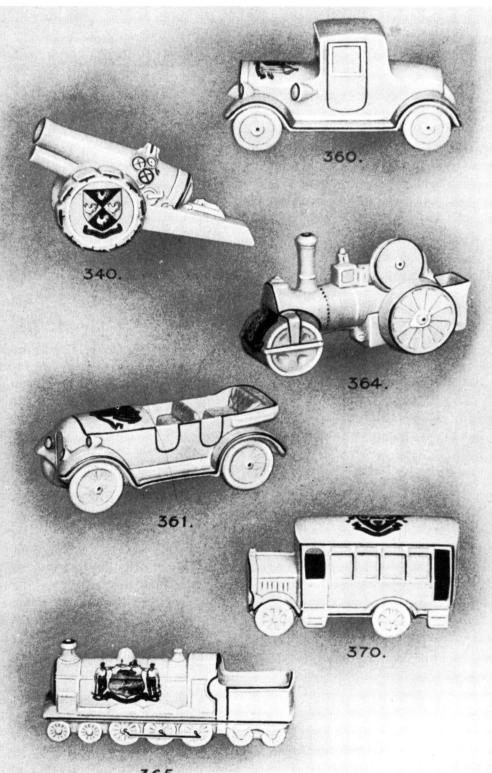

360.

340.

364.

361.

370.

365.

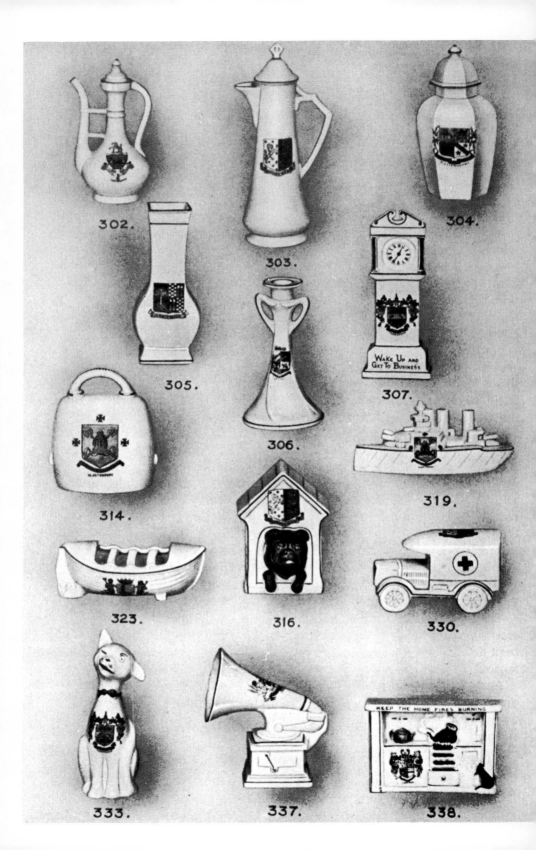

302.

303.

304.

305.

306.

307.

314.

319.

323.

316.

330.

333.

337.

338.

7½d. (3p) for simple shapes, up to 2s. 2d. (11p) for the liner *Aquitania* or an R.A.F. bi-plane.

As with most china firms who supplied heraldic china, Wileman & Co. also applied coats-of-arms to teaware, for example Dainty White or any of five other shapes, and to ashtrays or sweet dishes in a total of thirty-six shapes and sizes. Even shaving-mugs and butter-dishes could be embellished with a suitable souvenir feature. Another version of this line of merchandising was souvenir china and earthenware bearing engraved views of a particular place of interest.

The war had also stimulated the production of one form of pottery which it appears the firm never produced at any other time in its history. These were small busts of military figures who had risen to fame in that terrible era. Produced in Parian, the matt-finish unglazed porcelain commonly used in busts and statuettes, these pieces stood about 15 cm (6 in.) high. The only known examples are busts of Field Marshalls French and Kitchener, and the French General Joffre.

Happily for later generations of collectors a wider range of articles was made which celebrated more joyous and colourful occasions. At this point it also seems appropriate to detail the contribution made by Shelleys to the more usual forms of commemorative ware, by describing what can only be a small selection of this type of product.

Royal commemorations probably started with the 1887 examples for Queen Victoria's Golden Jubilee. These early designs were simple and the representations of royal persons were not always flattering. Rather more impressive, especially for Victoria's Diamond Jubilee in 1897, were the enamelled coats-of-arms and heraldic beasts which were available as alternatives to the portraits. The only problem with these, however, was that on teaware they accompanied a somewhat less impressive decoration, a bouquet of rose and thistle. The latter design did not last and by Edward VII's coronation in 1902, the royal standard and beasts were dominant. This made an unusually effective display on the Dainty White teaware.

The next two known designs, for George V's coronation in 1911 and his Silver Jubilee in 1935, reverted to a pattern which had also been available earlier, consisting of portraits of the King and Queen separated by a Union Jack.

In 1936, by way of preparation for the coronation of Edward VIII the following May, Shelleys brought out a more inventive yet still traditional range of commemorative china. About three dozen shapes and sizes were made, with a basic lithograph portrait of the king-to-be

31 Heraldic china from a catalogue, 1922

surrounded by laurels and Union Jacks. Different effects were achieved by applying graduated bands to the outside of pieces, especially large plates. While ashtrays were sold for 1s. 9d. (8½p) and large teapots for 5s. (25p), a specially designed two-handled china loving-cup was available at £1 1s. od. (£1.05). This also bore Edward's portrait but was embellished with gold handles and foot, and also bore a hand-painted spray of flowers. All pieces carried a special backstamp.

When Edward abdicated and a different coronation approached in 1937, the company produced at very short notice a completely new series with a significant change in design. Strongly featured were the loving-cups, now in three sizes, where the portraits of King George VI and Queen Elizabeth were surrounded by a modern wreath decoration, and the portraits of the royal children, Elizabeth and Margaret, appeared on the reverse. On the commemorative plates, either pair of portraits was again surrounded by the wreath in blue, but the wide border to the plate carried the inscription 'T.M. George VI and Elizabeth' in what could be termed a 'modern medieval' script, highlighted in gold. The overall effect was striking, modern and yet still regal. Also available were an earthenware lamp base in the same decoration, with a china shade, and a beer set consisting of six mugs with a musical jug which played the toast 'Here's health unto His Majesty' when raised.

Besides these royal commemoratives for the home market, the works produced a variety of wares commemorating a wide range of events in Britain and abroad. For example, a slender whisky flask with stopper produced in 1915 commemorated the centenary of the Battle of Waterloo, and bears portraits of Wellington and Kitchener against an all-over blue background of the Cloisello pattern.

The production of heraldic, souvenir and commemorative wares may have been at its height just after the 1914–18 war, but of course other areas of work were also developing. In some of his work Walter Slater continued to share the widespread enthusiasm for oriental styles. In the 1920s some department stores, such as Whiteley's, contained departments which specialized in oriental furnishings and artefacts: Chinese lanterns and lacquer furniture were the craze. At Wileman & Co. the Eastern influence already described in Intarsio, flambé and tea-ware patterns was carried on into lustre, cloisonné and other effects.

---

32 *opposite top*: Commemorative pieces, 1897, 1911, 1936

33 *opposite*: Commemorative wares from 1937

The first examples of lustre-decorated pieces were introduced in 1920. The technique used created a background of gradually changing colour on the piece, then ornamentation in gold and other colours was added, and finally a glaze with an irridescent finish. This is a completely different type of lustre decoration from that which involves the application of a thin coating of a metallic oxide, generally copper or silver. A more similar effect is probably mother-of-pearl glaze, which Wileman & Co. had used earlier, on white backgrounds. The particular glaze which creates this lustre effect — 'nitrate of bismuth dissolved in balsam of sulphur' — was patented by a Parisian chemist in about 1856, and examples of the technique were shown at the International Exhibition, London, in 1862. The lustre produced at Belleek and at Worcester was of a similar character. A serious drawback, however, especially with early pieces, was its tendency to lose brilliancy through ordinary use: in other words, it wears off.

Walter Slater's use of this style of decoration was probably most successful on the dark-coloured backgrounds he developed. A deep crimson at the neck of a vase, slowly changing to a deep blue at the base, or a steadily deepening shade of blue was used on many of the smaller china vases. The larger pieces generally featured single-colour backgrounds but with a greater amount of decoration. The large vase in colour plate V carries a complete scene in Japanese style and is signed by Walter Slater, as are a number of lustre pieces. Other examples include wide, shallow bowls called floating flower bowls: one with a golden galleon, white sails and conventionalized waves; another with opening water-lilies and a leaf motif in gold and green.

Another background colour used in lustre-decoration was sea-green. This was particularly effective for the silver or gold fish motifs

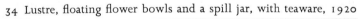

34 Lustre, floating flower bowls and a spill jar, with teaware, 1920

as in the hexagonal bowl illustrated in colour plate V. The Roumana style incorporated patterns with panels in blue, purple and orange, while other bowls were decorated with Celtic geometric patterns in gold and green on a variegated background.

Not all the lustre effects, therefore, adhered faithfully to the oriental style; indeed, the Vinta series of lustres used a vine and bluebird as the main subjects on an off-white background. Although the way the space is covered by branches and tendrils is reminiscent of Chinese decoration and some of the shapes used are strongly derivative of early Chinese ones, the overall impression of this series is decidedly English. By contrast the Blue Dragon pattern uses only true, oriental motifs: the Chinese dragon and flowers printed on a blue background under the lustre glaze look particularly striking on shapes such as ginger jars.

When such a variety of lustres was first introduced they found a welcoming public. At the 1921 British Industries Fair the whole of one side of Wileman & Co.'s display was devoted to these productions. During the customary royal visit, Queen Mary expressed particular interest and is reported to have referred to some of them as 'charming'. Their popularity was maintained through to about 1925, but when lustres were last mentioned in trade journals in 1928 only a few pieces were available.

A similar glaze was used at this time on wares which again used the Spano-Lustra label. In contrast to the earlier series of this name, which had used true lustres of the applied metallic variety, the new pieces used a lustre glaze over printed or stencilled designs.

A final type of decoration in this category again includes a number of examples signed by Walter Slater. This is the white, swirling fish motif on a green-grey background, shown in colour plate V. This design was also applied to many of the shapes in the lustre ware ranges.

In documenting the oriental-influenced wares it is noticeable that trade magazines of 1920 and 1921 made passing reference to *cloisonné* ware produced by Wileman & Co. *Cloisonné* is the term for a style of decoration used in China and Japan whereby a metal object is decorated by first soldering on wires to the required pattern. With this basis of relief work, the resulting spaces are filled with enamel, generally highly coloured. Thus a complex pattern of colours is achieved with separation by the metal wires. On pottery articles there are of course no soldered lines, but it seems likely that the term was used for highly

35 Oriental-style decanter probably designed by Frederick Rhead, 1915

coloured complex decorations where the colours were separated by lines, possibly in gold.

The Wileman version of *cloisonné* has been identified from a scrap in the pattern book. On either a black or deep-blue background an irregular pattern of lines was executed in white, rather like a Chinese 'crazy paving' pattern, and over this background bunches of coloured flowers were scattered. This style of decoration appeared on china and earthenware and was executed by a lithograph print registered in 1920. Sadly, no examples are known of which an illustration can be given.

While tracing *cloisonné*, another possible candidate presented itself from the registered designs. The decanter illustrated in plate 35 from 1915 is an impressive piece with obvious oriental influences, but again no examples are known. However, on closer inspection this design raises other questions. The scale-like repeating curves, especially on the handle, are reminiscent of patterns used in the first Intarsio range (see for example plate 6), and the central decoration is very similar to one used in the second Intarsio range, but only on pieces which have a rather different style from Walter Slater's general approach (spot the 'odd man out' in colour plate IV and in plate 25). Both these elements featured very strongly in the work being produced by Frederick Rhead at Wood & Sons' subsidiary which made Bursley ware, especially the Bagdad range. It seems likely, then, that examples of Frederick's designs were being introduced long after he had left Wileman & Co.

In china teaware Walter continued the themes already described in ornamental ware. One of the most successful of the immediately post-war patterns was called Indian Peony. This featured a black, printed branch motif with leaves and a flower in enamelled green, and is a fine example of the high quality which was possible using this 'print and enamel' technique of decoration. The strength of colour used on this pattern led the *Pottery Gazette* to comment on the 'peculiarly rich colour, with quite a degree of body in it – what one usually understands in the trade as a "fat" green'. Besides the china teaware in the Gainsborough shape, Indian Peony was also applied to vases and ornaments and in these cases also featured a mother-of-pearl glaze. The small vase illustrated in plate 36 is shaped in the style of seventeenth-century Chinese vases.

At first the pattern Indian Peony was reserved for Soane & Smith, a store in London's Oxford Street. It was a design which was to remain popular, and despite the ease with which its allegiances changed (this

36 Indian Peony pattern on earthenware and china, c. 1918

Indian pattern on a Chinese shape was at one time called 'Persian'), it remained in production until the 1940s, some variants being called Ovington and others Chippendale.

The oriental influence was waning, however. Perhaps its generally romantic appeal did not fit easily with the reality of the early 1920s. The post-war boom had been short-lived, private investment in the Stock Exchange had collapsed after earlier enormous profits, and by June 1921 more than two million people were unemployed. In that year pottery workers accepted a decrease in earnings. At the annual 'settling day' between workers and employers the piece-work rates were lowered 'to ease prices'. The period was also marked by much less advertising on the part of pottery firms: Wileman & Co.'s advertisements in trade magazines served to announce that they would not be showing at trade fairs. Wileman & Co. had already been described as catering for 'what one might describe as the upper middle-class trade . . . in these days of high prices, when it is undoubtedly difficult to meet the purse of the working classes'. In a society where these class divisions were still strong, a pottery firm needed to consider carefully its prospects for trade. Other divisions were growing amongst the

37 Jack and Eileen, Bob and Doris at their wedding, 1923

population. In contrast to the 'new rich' who had made money during the war, many of the middle-class viewed themselves as the 'new poor'. True, the number of domestic servants had been greatly reduced, but life in the suburbs still involved buying new cars and other consumer goods. More important for the potteries, it still involved the traditions of afternoon tea and of valuing fine china, and the tastes expressed by the buying public showed traces of pre-war elegance at the same time as new experimentation.

The number of shapes being produced in teaware at this stage was quite considerable. Eleven styles were available, including three which Percy Shelley had introduced in about 1919, named after his sons – Norman, Vincent and Kenneth shapes.

For the three sons, the early 1920s were not such a time of hardship as they were for those from less fortunate families. For (Vincent) Bob and (Kenneth) Jack, the identical twins whom even their mother was unable to distinguish at times (although as they grew older they looked less similar, and are also reported to have developed distinctly different characters), these years involved activities such as motoring in the new MG sports car and dancing at the grand hotels of resorts along the North Wales coast. It was at one such hotel in Llandudno that they met a pair of friends, Doris Hammersley and Eileen Nelson – a meeting which led to a double wedding at Alsager in 1923, which created much local interest. The couples returned from their honeymoons to a pair of identical houses which had been built for them in Barlaston Road.

The eldest brother, Norman, had meanwhile been more concerned with his golf, his poultry farm and his interest in breeding dogs. He married in 1932 Margery Bailey, eldest daughter of Kenneth Bailey who was a manager at Doulton's Nile Street Works, Burslem.

The positive effect of the sons' contribution to the activity of the pottery continued and developed. On the production side the bone china body was achieving very high quality results. This was enhanced by the fact that the thickness of the china in shapes such as cups had been reduced in new designs, with the result that the phrase 'eggshell china' was commonly applied to Shelley wares. It was always said that Percy Shelley made a secret of the exact recipe for his bone china: some variation in the ingredients is possible and small changes in the amount of bone included can have significant results. Percy used a larger than average amount of bone which he bought himself, as he did not trust the normal supplies of ground bone from those firms which served the pottery industry. At this time also, the firm made its own glazes, a practice which eventually disappeared from many potteries as specialist firms developed.

Improvements were not only evident in the quality of production: the overall organization of the works was redesigned for greater efficiency and many labour-saving practices were introduced. Indeed, it became more common for reviewers of the firm's products to comment on their management than their wares. 'The counting-house arrangements of this firm would surprise many', and reference to 'certain systems of official referenda' led the Pottery Gazette to inform its readers of 'a pottery which stands in a different category from the ordinary run of Staffordshire potteries'. The showroom was described in 1925 as one of the best appointed in the Potteries.

This progressive outlook may well have helped towards Shelleys' survival and success in the difficult years which were approaching. This period of the firm's production is possibly the best known to many people, yet it was economically one of the most problematic.

As though in anticipation, Wileman & Co. changed their name, found larger modern showrooms in London, greatly increased all forms of advertising and produced more inventive wares.

6

A pottery named Shelleys

On 1 January 1925 the firm which had been managed by members of the Shelley family for over fifty years first bore their name. Announcements read: 'There is no useful purpose served by using the name Wileman any longer' and the firm became titled Shelleys. The trademark was at last registered.

The London showrooms which had first been at Holborn Circus and then, in the hands of Tom E. Taylor, had moved to Holborn Viaduct, were now transferred to Holborn itself under the charge of John Sayer. Sayer had earlier been a representative for Wood & Sons, Bursley Limited, and Birks, Rawlins & Co., but now left these positions to his brother Ebenezer in order to represent Belleek and others at the new Shelley address. He was also developing a considerable reputation as a designer of display stands for china. Shelleys maintained showrooms in the then important colonial markets: Sydney and Melbourne, Australia; Auckland, New Zealand; Durban, South Africa.

Advertising, which had been kept to a minimum, was now increased greatly in both amount and form, probably on Jack's advice. An advertising agency, Smedley Services, was engaged and their results were striking (see chapter 8).

None of this organization would have been effective, however, if the firm had not produced wares which were attractive to the public eye. Before considering Shelleys' successes in bone china let us consider their pre-eminence at that time in two rather different areas: nursery ware and domestic china.

Since 1902 Wileman & Co. had produced wares specially for child-ren's use. These were simple illustrations of well-known nursery rhymes printed on to feeding bowls, plates and dishes. Before the First World War some of these had achieved popularity, especially series known as Peter Pan, Boy Scouts and Puff Puff. In 1918 a more modern set of illustrations was introduced using lithographic printing rather than engraving and transfer prints. This series was called Bryta nursery ware. The themes of these illustrations were still popular nursery rhymes such as 'The Old Woman Who Lived in a Shoe'. Probably a large number of potteries were producing children's wares of these types with simple decoration from traditional themes.

In 1925, however, Shelleys broke away from that tradition and started a line of successes which continued for many years to come. For in that year they employed a well-known illustrator of the period, Hilda Cowham, to provide decorations for nursery ware. The results were significantly different from previous examples in two ways. First, the style of illustration was one which would in theory appeal specifi-cally to children. It was simple and stylized, rather than being elaborate and 'realistic' like Edwardian examples, such as William Savage Cooper's designs for Doulton's. Second, the content of the illustrations had moved away from the traditional nursery rhyme themes with their implicit moral messages, to a simple representation of children's activities. This series was called Playtime.

It is not known whether it was as a result of this series' great success or the lack of it that a second illustrator was engaged, and one year later another series was launched bearing a name which was to be known by millions – Mabel Lucie Attwell. Mabel Lucie (1879–1964) had not been inspired by an academic art training and from about 1900 she had started to illustrate children's books. Her style was originally one involving slender waif-like figures, and the chubby, cheeky, pre-cocious characters for which she is best known developed gradually. By 1906 she designed posters for the London Underground, and she did so again in 1917. From 1910–19 commissions for advertising came from Vim, Swan Fountain Pens, Blueband Margarine and others, while her illustrated books and postcards started their long-standing success.

Mabel Lucie Attwell knew she was designing for adult buyers. Her intention was to portray particular aspects of childhood to adults, and in so doing she used situations and language which were not represen-tative of children but which embodied an adult view of them. Her work had the flavour of those moments when adults laugh at children's

38 Nursery ware design by Mabel Lucie Attwell, 1926

incongruous behaviour: the children do not laugh because they do not understand, and Mabel Lucie knew it.

When she first began to design for Shelleys she had recently had published a number of books featuring a species of small elf in green suits, the 'Boo Boos'. When the first six designs for plates were registered in June 1926 they portrayed scenes involving children, Boo Boos and animals, each scene being accompanied by a few lines of verse. For example, one illustration shows a chubby young boy in a small cart being drawn by a donkey. The cart is loaded with a representative bunch of green-suited elves and the verse reads:

> We've just come from fairy-land
> With our donkey small
> Sometimes he will go quite fast
> And sometimes not at all.

39 Nursery ware design by Hilda Cowham, 1927

A few months later the accompanying teaset was launched. This again showed that Shelleys were not tied to tradition in nursery ware, for instead of the common practice of applying nursery decorations to standard tea shapes, Shelleys produced distinctively modelled shapes. The teapot is a mushroom house, the sugar-bowl another spotted mushroom and the milk-jug is none other than a Boo Boo, standing in a coy saluting pose so that one can lift him by the elbow and pour milk from his head (see colour plate VIIIa).

The response to these creations was enthusiastic. The *Pottery Gazette* wrote of 'a truly irresistible range of nursery ware, altogether in advance of what was usually put before the trade'. Whether today's observers regard them as a horrendous form of kitsch or as lovable examples of pottery, the fact is that they sold very well.

Indeed, the success of Mabel Lucie Attwell ware led to an improvement in Hilda Cowham ware. In August 1927 a new series of designs for plates was registered, displaying a much bolder style of illustration, and in 1928 the teaware was on the market, again featuring innovative shapes: the teapot was a green bathing tent, the sugar-bowl was a seaside pail and the milk-jug a shell with a seaweed handle (see colour plate VIIIb). The teapot is a classic piece of nursery nonsense, but the quality of modelling is remarkable. By present tastes it might have been

40 Mabel Lucie Attwell Animal series, 1930

expected that this Hilda Cowham series would prove equal to Mabel Lucie Attwell's, but on the evidence of the number of known pieces remaining in existence, it was produced in considerably smaller numbers. Complete sets are extremely rare.

The success of Mabel Lucie Attwell's teaset may have been too much for Hilda Cowham's designs, but it did not stop Shelleys introducing other alternatives. In 1930 the Mabel Lucie Attwell Animal series was first made, and advertised as an additional line 'for those kiddies who will have animals and nothing else'. The *Pottery and Glass Record* commented rather succinctly: 'the cream-jug is in the form of a comic rabbit, the teapot a quaint duck and the sugar a grotesque chicken. These are brightly coloured.' Again, judging by present rarity, this series was not produced in large numbers.

By 1928 Shelleys had considerable competition from other potters for that style of nursery ware decorated by well-known illustrators. Paragon had employed Beatrice Mallett, Ashtead Potters used Winnie the Pooh illustrations by F. H. Shepard, Hammersley depicted Lewis Carroll themes with the Sir John Tenniel drawings, and Midwinter scooped Heath Robinson to portray traditional nursery rhymes. Nevertheless, no other examples are known from this time in which complete shapes were modelled, that is, in which the decoration and shape

41 Mabel Lucie Attwell baby plate, mug and chamberpot, c. 1934

incorporated each other. Perhaps Shelleys avoided the attention of copyists by their judicious registering of designs: a registered design number appeared on the base of each piece of the three, modelled tea-sets. What other potteries may not have known was that only the first Mabel Lucie Attwell set was in fact registered – the numbers from that registration were freely used on the other sets.

It was the first Mabel Lucie Attwell style which continued in popu-larity during the 1930s. By 1934, nearly thirty different pieces were available including mugs, beakers, plates, cups and saucers in china; and plates, the teaset, a cruet set and chamber-pot in earthenware. In 1936 the 'Sleepy-head' nightlight was introduced, alongside the orange squeezer, a choice of sizes in chamber-pot, and that necessary addition for many children – the covered plate which kept food warm by containing hot water in its base. 1937 saw the appearance of the covered jug and the serviette ring, and the demise of the green pixie jug, which was replaced by a traditional shape decorated as the mush-room sugar-bowl.

In fact, the late 1930s saw a general decline in Boo Boos. They appeared less frequently on plate patterns and when a series of Mabel Lucie Attwell statuettes was originated in 1937, the fairy subjects gave pride of place to figures of precocious children (see colour plate IX). The largest, 'Our Pets', was approximately 20 cm (8 in.) high, whereas the range of about a dozen single figures stood at approximately 15 cm (6 in.). These included characters which Mabel Lucie Attwell had made famous in other areas, such as 'Diddums' and 'The Toddler'. Any of these figures could also be supplied fitted as a table lamp. The smallest figures included elves peeping round mushrooms and sitting on puppies' backs. Eight were initially produced, but this series was developed after the 1939–45 war and eventually included 'The Mushroom Village' and 'The Little Mermaid'.

Mabel Lucie Attwell continued to submit designs to Shelleys for many years, either introducing new sets of illustrations or replacing those which were not selling well. The modelled teasets were not produced after the 1939–45 war, but china plates, bowls, mugs and so on were available, along with the small china figures. The competition, however, was becoming progressively stronger, especially after 1934 which brought Doulton's introduction of Bunnykins nursery ware designed by Barbara Vernon Bailey, a relative of Norman Shelley's wife Margery Bailey.

Children's ware, therefore, was one of the lines which helped Shelleys through the late twenties and early thirties, by appealing to those middle-class parents who shared the view of childhood enshrined therein. For less well-off members of the community the cheaper wares produced by Shelleys in that period may have proved attractive and within reach. These included domestic ware or white ware in a very wide range.

A catalogue for domestic ware from about 1930 illustrates over four hundred different shapes and sizes, in both china and earthenware, the latter euphemistically titled 'semi-porcelain'. Domestic pottery had been produced since the 1890s and the range which developed included many pieces of specialized ware. Comports, covered muffin dishes, multiple cake trays and menu stands in china accompanied cucumber trays, fish dishes and drainers, hot-water covered bacon dishes and pie funnels in earthenware. Even table-spoons, dessert-spoons and tea-spoons were made. Fifty-four different sweet dishes, ashtrays or butter-dishes in china and some jugs in nine different sizes must have made choice rather difficult.

Another fifty shapes and sizes in plain white earthenware made up a range for which the firm was perhaps better known. These were the Shelley jelly moulds. Starting in about 1904 the series was different from most of those produced by competitors. The outstanding feature was that the shape on the inside of the mould was reproduced on the outside, instead of the outside being the usual nondescript form. One advantage of this was that buyers could easily see the shape that should result, without having to imagine the inversion as they peered inside.

A Fine TURNOUT

Agents:
AUSTRALIA : T. W. Heath & Co. Ltd., 232, Clarence St., Sydney, and Commerce House, Melbourne, N.S.W.
NEW ZEALAND : Thos. Webb & Co. Ltd., Ormiston Buildings, Albert Street, Auckland.
SOUTH AFRICA : J. W. Hutty, Hulston's Buildings, Smith Street, Durban. Also at Cape Town.

The Shelley Jelly Moulds we offer you have a valuable and distinctive feature which will appeal to the Housewife. They are *uniform* in thickness of Earthenware all over the patterned decoration, a deter= mining factor in turning out the Jelly easily and whole.

This is a strong selling point and will make a satisfied customer. We make these Moulds in a great variety of shapes.

May we send you a complete folder, illustrating the various shapes and sizes of our Jelly Moulds ?

Shelley MOULDS

London Showrooms : 14/18, Holborn, E.C.1.

SHELLEYS (Formerly Wileman & Co.) LONGTON
STOKE—ON—TRENT.

42 Advertisement for jelly moulds, 1925

ACANTHUS

ARMADILLO

CRAYFISH

ROUND ORNAMENTAL

STAR.

RITZ

QUEENS

CARLTON
SMALL CREAM CENTRE.

FRENCH

FLUTED BOWL

CECIL (SURROUND ONLY)

SAVOY (CREAM CENTRE)

43 Twelve of the eighteen jelly mould shapes, 1922

But more important was the theory that with an equal thickness of earthenware at all parts of the mould, heat would travel evenly when it came to loosening the jelly and a perfect result would be achieved. This was also helped by a high quality finish.

Each of the fifteen shapes was given a name: some were the names of hotels such as Ritz, Savoy, Carlton and Queens; others were the names of areas such as Westminster and Victoria; while Armadillo and Crayfish were self-explanatory. Most were available in four different sizes, the largest and most ornate costing 2s. (10p), and some were available in an individual size costing 5d. (2p). In 1933 the addition of three sizes of Rabbit, Hen and Swan brought the total available to fifty-nine, but none of them was available after the 1939–45 war, when earthenware production ceased at Shelley Potteries and the tea-tables of Britain were less often graced with such delicately-shaped confections.

Shelleys also produced a variety of appliances for hospital use, but probably the most appealing are the wedge-shaped bed slippers produced for Boots the chemists. They carry the advice that extra comfort will be afforded the patient by placing a piece of flannel over the appliance before placing it under the patient. These were produced from 1920 to about 1930. Other non-domestic white ware had earlier included printing and fixing trays for the photographic trade.

Last in this review of the products which not only helped trade through the difficult 1920s but also allowed the firm to develop as an active expanding company, comes a line which was of great importance to many pottery firms. This was ware with which other companies advertised their products. Shelleys had created a link with whisky firms in particular as early as 1910, when ashtrays, match-strikers and other 'bar furniture' were produced for White Horse. At their peak the orders from whisky firms comprised 100,000 jugs and 200,000 ashtrays! The ashtrays were designed so that two could be packed inside a jug. Customers included Black and White, Highland Queen, White Horse, John Haig and Booths Gin, together with breweries such as William Youngers, Worthington and Shepherd Neame. The early pieces are identifiably Shelley; they bear the firm's backstamp and use decorations which had also been used on teaware, such as the blue snakeskin transfer on the match-striker illustrated in plate 44. In the 1920s, however, when the trade in advertising ware was considerable, a simple 'Made in England' backstamp was used and the shape and decoration of many pieces bore no resemblance to Shelleys' other productions.

44 Advertising ware: match striker, c. 1912; ashtray, c. 1930; jug, c. 1934

Some novelty shapes were modelled, such as an ashtray in the shape of a horse's hoof for White Horse, but in the 1930s this trade declined and earthenware production was given over to other lines. Some of the few remaining advertising wares then became more identifiably Shelley again, as the Bulloch Lade whisky jug illustrated in plate 44 reveals.

There are interesting comparisons to be made between this period and the difficult economic situation in the 1890s. In the earlier period Percy Shelley had just joined the firm and his energy encouraged it to grow and develop. Now the joint efforts of other new members led the company to expand and diversify, while elsewhere others struggled and failed. The economic climate also raised other parallels with earlier times. Towards the close of 1923 Stanley Baldwin, who was soon to become Prime Minister, revived the protectionist attitude towards trade policy. Under the new title of 'safeguarding of industry' this attitude attracted just as much criticism from Percy Shelley as the earlier ver-

46 Bob, Jack, Percy and Norman at the works, c. 1930

sions had done. He described attempts to impose duties on foreign pottery as short-sighted and narrow. At a Chamber of Commerce meeting he stated that although he was connected with the Longton china trade, which had never made any money and never would, he did not want to look through the wrong end of a telescope and he was afraid that a good many of his protectionist friends frequently did just that by only wanting to protect their own narrow interests.

Percy also maintained his previous attitude towards his employees and the growth of trade unionism. When the General Strike came in 1926, he called his potters out on the first day of the strike and all of them went on the dole. At this time the polarization between owners and workers was increased, and styles of management tended to be harsh. Percy's liberal attitude was in marked contrast to that of many potters. When he decided to retain a printer who had been fined for

45 Percy Shelley photographed c. 1930

stealing wares from the factory, the trade press found it worthy of being reported, describing Percy as 'magnanimous'.

Notwithstanding his continuing strength of feeling on these matters, Percy was nearing seventy years of age and had been proprietor of the pottery for almost fifty years. The three young men of the next generation were given greater formal responsibility in January 1929 when the limited company, Shelley Potteries, was formed with father and three sons as equal shareholders. The assets of Shelleys at that time were valued at over £58,000.

Percy retired from active participation in the business in 1932, moved to Bournemouth, and after about two years of illness he died in 1937. During his career he had firmly established the position of Shelleys in twentieth-century pottery. He left behind him a tradition and a reputation for high quality china, and no doubt had directly and indirectly influenced many others towards his view that there was nothing as beautiful as good china.

He did not, however, leave behind as buoyant a state of affairs at the works as had existed some years previously. In 1933, only one year after Percy's retirement, Jack had died in hospital following an abdominal operation. Although he was not regarded as a strong man, this came as a considerable shock. It also came at a time when Jack's particular contribution to the firm was bearing fruit. He had been instrumental in initiating what was to be a successful advertising campaign (see chapter 8), a particularly bold move in depressed times, and earlier in the year of his death the firm had at last broken its run of non-appearances at the British Industries Fair – something Jack would have supported.

The 1930s also witnessed a decline in the influence of Walter Slater on the firm's products. Having indelibly made his impression on Shelley wares, he slowly handed over responsibility to his son Eric. By 1938 he had retired from the company, and he died soon after.

❧ 7 ❧

A high-point in style

Although the diverse wares which have been described above no doubt contributed greatly to the firm's survival, it was the fine bone china wares which created the firm's public reputation. For many people the name Shelley is synonymous with delicate teaware of the 1920s and 1930s.

One of the best-known shapes produced in this period is Queen Anne. This is characterized by an octagonal design, the cups, bowls, jugs and pots having four large panels and four small panels forming their sides (see colour plate VII). This shape was in fact a remodelling of an earlier shape which Wileman's had created around the turn of the century. The earlier version had included regular octagonal plates but these were later replaced by square plates with a suggestion of an octagonal shape in the ribbing at each corner. The design of some pieces, particularly the milk-jug, was almost identical. Perhaps because of its predecessor, Queen Anne was at first called the Antique shape, but no doubt this was deemed unsuitable for an era with an increasing emphasis on modernity. In August 1926 the shape was registered with the Design Registry and the first patterns were entered in the company's pattern book.

Queen Anne was quite a new departure for Shelleys. Previous to this the shapes in teaware which were produced by moulding were Dainty and Oleander, both of which were ornate traditional styles. Queen Anne presented a much less cluttered look. It was also introduced at a time when the more ordinary 'turned' shapes were proving successful, especially the Vincent shape – a standard cylindrical form with a slightly flared rim and small foot.

The patterns which were applied to the Queen Anne shape demonstrated how delicate the effect obtained by the 'print and enamel' style of decoration could be. At first the patterns featured bunches of fruit or flowers, but not portrayed in a classical manner. Rather they were combined with small backgrounds or borders in such a way as to make maximum effect of the panelled shape. The Blue Iris pattern, no. 11561 (see colour plate VIIa), is a good example from 1927 and was popular for a number of years. The representation of natural subjects became more and more stylized, as in the Black Leafy Tree pattern, no. 11575 (see colour plate VIIb).

This trend was somewhat altered by the introduction of a series of designs which had a fortuitous start. Eric Slater had been on a visit to London at the time of a Buckingham Palace garden party and on passing the window of a large store had been inspired by a photograph of the event. He went directly back to his hotel and created in watercolours the design which became Archway of Roses, pattern no. 11606 (see colour plate VIIa). Soon to follow were a series called Garden Scenes and a number of designs featuring cottages of various sorts (see no. 11621 in colour plate VIIb). On their introduction in 1928 these patterns were warmly received and sold well for a couple of years. They contrasted strongly with the earlier effects, since not only was the representation more naturalistic, but also the geometry of the shape was often completely ignored.

A third type of ornamentation may have been stimulated by the ever-deepening economic depression of those years. The 'print and enamel' technique is a very labour-intensive one, requiring engravers, printers, transferers and decorators who may be using up to six different colours in enamel. The main alternative technique is the use of lithographic printed patterns which had always been used, especially on cheaper wares. In the 1920s, however, this tradition had been dying out, with only a third of the previous proportion of patterns using lithography. Nevertheless, in 1929 Shelleys introduced the Crabtree litho, pattern no. 11651 (see colour plate VIIb) and found yet another success for the Queen Anne shape.

Probably the most successful of all the patterns for Queen Anne, and there were over 170, was one of the latest. This was no. 11678, Sunset and Tall Trees, which was introduced in late 1929 (see colour plate VIIb). It no doubt appealed to many people's romanticism with regard

47 Queen Anne shape teaware, with cottage pattern, 1928

to the country, and was the longest-surviving design to be applied, still being featured in the firm's retail catalogues in 1935. It was also one of the most popular patterns for a new venture in Queen Anne ware – matching earthenware dinner services.

Although Shelleys had been making dinnerware for many years, this was almost entirely in china, most of which had been for export and even less of which would have been used for its supposed function. They were known as 'course plates' and were intended for decoration only. However, by the later 1920s Percy Shelley seems to have been sufficiently confident about his manufacture of white earthenware ('semi-porcelain') to begin producing dinner services to match the beautifully white bone china tea and coffee services. Coverdishes, serving plates and sauceboats were designed in the Queen Anne shape, and for a number of the styles available customers could purchase complete services.

New patterns for Queen Anne were not introduced after July 1933 (with the exception of an unsuccessful attempt at reintroduction in the later 1950s), although, as has been mentioned, several of the already existing designs carried on in production until some time later. One final variant which is worthy of mention was stimulated by a development in the Dainty White range. In 1932 a series of Dainty Floral patterns had been introduced, in which small flowers and leaves were moulded into the top of the handle of each piece. These were coloured, to match any other decoration that might be applied. Perhaps this turned out to be a successful line, for in the same year Queen Anne Floral was created, in which the handles were in the form of a tulip and its stem. Only three patterns were produced in this style.

To refer to Queen Anne Floral as a separate line may suggest that there was little variety in the main range: this would be a false impression. There were two distinct proportions of cup, 'tall and low'; and three sizes, coffee, tea and 'afternoon tea'. Teapots, coffee-pots, open jugs and covered jugs were each available in three sizes ranging from one to two pints in capacity. These were listed in a somewhat unusual way, referred to as 'the potter's count', which was related to the number of pieces that could be placed in a particular size of kiln. Thus the smallest capacity was termed '36s' and the largest '12s'. Various compositions of sets were on offer, teasets, coffee sets, morning sets, sandwich sets and so on. In about 1929 a complete coffee set could be bought for just over £2.

Shelleys' Queen Anne range had captured the attention of the buying public for almost ten years, no doubt because of its stylish lines and wide variety of patterns. It had also proved itself on the export markets, the Australian agent in particular describing it as 'a huge success'. Such a success attracted the efforts of Japanese imitators: exact replicas of the teaware were produced in a much poorer quality china. Most were directed towards Australia but some found their way to Britain.

As an aside, it is worthwhile noting that Shelleys themselves were not above being accused of imitating. In about 1928 the products of William Moorcroft captured Eric Slater's attention: the deep-coloured fruit executed in tube-lining on a deep-blue background was proving a popular and tasteful decoration. He suggested to his father that a similar style in bas-relief rather than tube-lining would be attractive, so they created a number of pieces with fruit shapes raised from the body, and the necessary moulds were made. Earthenware articles were produced, coloured in similar tones to those of Moorcroft, and began to be marketed. Within a week Moorcroft himself was in touch with Percy Shelley, promising dire consequences if the production continued. Percy had no wish to create conflict with another manufacturer,

48 Shelley pieces in the style of W. Moorcroft, c. 1929

and was mindful of the Manufacturers' Federation's view about copying, so this particular line died a sudden death.

The wide range of Queen Anne patterns may have been a result of the fact that there were at the time three Slaters working in the studio. Walter's younger son, Kenneth, worked for Shelleys for a few years before emigrating to Canada with his new wife Clara Knight, a designer and decorator. But it is a study of the older brother, Eric, which provides an understanding of the next development in bone china productions.

Although the Queen Anne shape had proved popular in the late 1920s, the state of trade was not improving and other attempts to increase sales were needed, even though the proportion of the population who were buying bone china was probably dwindling. Eric Slater was

49 Walter Slater, Eric Slater and Clara Knight in the studio, c. 1930

reaching his full confidence as a designer in about 1930, but despite successes such as Archway of Roses, he (along with many other designers of his generation) was increasingly frustrated by copying styles from the past. The 1920s had been a period of ambivalence, with much promise of modernism but without an equivalent realization, especially in the pottery industry where new influences in design often came later than in fabrics, metalwork or furniture.

In 1930 Eric created a pair of shapes which were ultra-modern in conception and strikingly different from anything that the firm had produced previously. These were given the names Vogue and Mode (see colour plates X and XI). The conical form with solid triangular handles was one of the strongest geometric designs of that style which is now known as Art Deco. Even though competitors created similar shapes in bone china, especially Paragon's Duchess of 1931, Wedgwood's Farnol of 1935 and Brain's Foley Mayfair range, and others produced parallels in earthenware, such as Clarice Cliff's Conical shape (registered in 1931), Shelleys' impact was strengthened by the high quality bone china and the striking patterns which were applied to complement the medium rather than conflict with it.

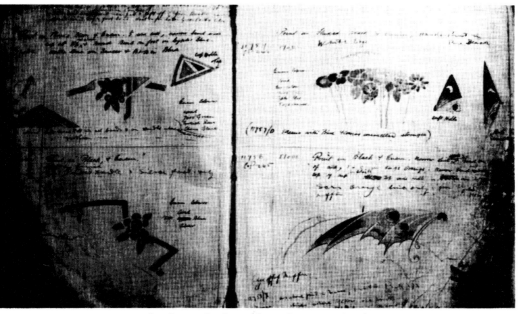

50 Patterns for the Mode shape, from the pattern book, 1930

Vogue and Mode shapes differed in the amount of tapering in their conical sections. Vogue was the wider of the two at the rim, and tapered steeply to the base and a noticeable foot. Both were made in tea and coffee sizes and of course were 'turned' shapes, that is, the potting was completed on a lathe where excess clay was shaved from the outside reducing the piece to the correct thickness – in the case of Vogue cups, just over 1 mm.

Patterns started with up-dated and more geometric versions of the band and flower motif style, for example the red J pattern, no. 11739 (see colour plate XI). The first group of designs included one motif which was not only successful in its own time, but which has come to be seen as one of the characteristics of the thirties and is one of Shelleys' most illustrated works. This is Sunray, no. 11742 (see colour plate X, and variants in colour plate XI). The 1930 buyer would have paid £2 8s. 9d. (£2.44) for a twenty-one-piece Vogue teaset in this style. Other patterns on the Vogue shape were sometimes more expensive, especially where the use of gold or silver was involved. The Mode shape was slightly less expensive, a twenty-one-piece teaset in Butterfly Wing, no. 11758 (see colour plate XI), was £2 0s. 6d. (£2.02½) whereas

a complete coffee set in no. 11755 as illustrated in plate 51 was £1 11s. 2d. (£1.56).

When first introduced, Eric's efforts met with a guarded reception. The *Pottery Gazette* wrote: 'They may or may not carry the public by storm, but one thing they certainly will do, they will cause people to stop and think . . . There are those who for a long time past have been agitating for a more adventurous spirit in the manufacturing circles of the pottery trade. Well here it is!' True, the call for change had been long-standing: in the late 1920s Royal Society of Arts competitions for designs had caused the pottery judges to remark on 'the almost complete lack of originality . . . the tendency to cling to present and past practice, and no suggestion of fresh ideas'. Gordon Forsyth had reviewed the pottery section of the 1925 Paris Exhibition in fairly scathing tones. Yet when the call was answered the response was equivocal.

A later group of patterns took the geometric style a stage further: various combinations of rectangles, sometimes overlapping, formed the central motifs (see examples in colour plate XI). However, the Vogue shape was not to be a lasting success. The last pattern was introduced in 1932, there having been forty-nine in all but taken from only twenty-three distinct designs, various colour combinations being listed as separate patterns.

The policy of producing matching dinnerware in earthenware was also applied to the Vogue shape. A new coverdish and sauceboat were modelled with cubist handles, and the fashion of square plates was continued in three sizes (see colour plate Xb).

The Vogue shape was unpopular for two of its main design features. The wide shape allowed tea to cool too quickly for some customers' liking and the solid handle brought a variety of comments. Buyers complained that they could not place a finger through the handle: Eric's reply was that no tea-drinker would really do this on a cup with a ring handle. Other complained that the cups could not be hung up on their usual hooks: Shelleys' reply was, 'we fear we shall have to somehow manage to bore holes through this very attractive handle'. And this, effectively, is what they did. In March 1932 the Eve shape was introduced, and although it was first called New Vogue it was more of a development from the Mode shape since it had the narrower style of cup. The last of only thirty-one patterns on Mode was entered in 1931, and the Eve shape was allowed to carry on the style with its open handle, examples being produced throughout the late thirties and even one or two after the 1939–45 war. Again, a matching series of dinner-

51 *opposite top*: Coffee sets in the Mode shape, 1930

52 *opposite*: Teaset in the Eve shape, 1932

ware was modelled, a twenty-six-piece set in the style illustrated in plate 53 costing £4 11s. 6d. (£4.57½) in 1935, when the same size service in Queen Anne shape was costing three guineas.

At first it may seem surprising that such startling styles were produced by a china firm in the early 1930s. Those were the darkest days of the depression with over 20% of the registered working population unemployed. The effects of the Wall Street Crash were indirect for the British people but they lasted through to 1935. The most immediate effect for a firm like Shelleys was the virtual collapse of the American market, so that an increase in sales was necessary on the home front. Cheaper wares, therefore, were required to appeal to more home buyers. Some Mode teasets were half the cost of Queen Anne shapes, but what made Shelleys risk such extreme designs? Critics of mid-1920s design seemed now to have much more practical force to their argument that a greater attention to the artistic side of industry was required. The slogan now was 'design or decline', so when Eric Slater presented his new styles it is likely that their reception would have been more optimistic than might first be imagined. From what is known about Jack Shelley, he would probably have supported a high-risk strategy to increase sales. Perhaps it was already recognized that ultra-modern shapes would have a shorter period of success.

By the time Vogue and Mode were no longer being developed, a new shape was going into production which was to prove of longer-lasting appeal to the public and was to consolidate Eric Slater's reputation as a designer in the eyes of his colleagues. In September 1932 the Regent shape demonstrated a move from all straight lines to all curves, the flared trumpet shape being complemented by the perfect circle of the ring handles (see colour plates XII and XIII). Not only was this an appealing design visually, but it also proved a very practical design, easy to hold, well balanced, and comfortable to drink from. Some time later, Gordon Forsyth, by now regarded by many as the most powerful influence in pottery design, selected the Regent shape to illustrate good design in his book 20th Century Ceramics: an international survey of the best work . . .

The patterns applied again showed changes in style. The first was a blue flower pattern called Syringa and soon there followed the very popular Anemone Bunch (both illustrated in the foreground of colour plate XII). Whereas the earlier patterns on the Queen Anne shape had shown how delicate the 'print and enamel' technique could be with small flowers, these designs showed that floral subjects could be treated

53 Dinnerware in the Eve shape, 1934

boldly by the same technique. This difference was partly achieved by utilizing the print to form either part of the main motif or a background to it, instead of merely using the print to provide an outline for the enameller, as had been done previously. Thus it became common for the leaves in a floral motif to be applied at the print stage, and this opened up the possibility of achieving significantly different results by printing in different coloured inks. Black, brown, grey, green, blue, mauve, gold, and various mixtures were used.

These patterns were well-favoured when in 1933 Shelleys made their comeback to exhibiting at the British Industries Fair. 'The designs were characteristically free in their conception and the colours fresh and appealing', wrote one reviewer. Regent appeared alongside Eve, Queen Anne (still the Sunset pattern) and Floral Dainty, backed by a display of the 'very striking and richly coloured artware' called Harmony.

Perhaps the return to exhibiting in 1933 explains the sudden increase in the number of patterns created that year when the depression was at its worst. Nearly 180 were entered, as compared with an average of 80 per year for the previous five years. By the summer of 1933 and the Exhibition of Industrial Art at Dorland Hall, examples of new geometrical designs on the Regent shape were ready. This exhibition was largely organized by the Design and Industries Association in response to a government report recommending greater publicity for the best products of contemporary design, and led to the larger exhibitions at Burlington House in later years. The selection committees read like a *Who's Who* of contemporary design: Wells Coates, Serge Chermayeff, E. McKnight Kauffer and Oliver Hill were variously engaged to ensure that this would be an exhibition of exceptionally high standard. The pottery and glass selection committee included Raymond McGrath and was chaired by Gordon Forsyth.

Catalogues and reviews suggest that Shelley Potteries selected five teasets, but in fact six managed to find their way on to the small stand. Eve and Regent shapes were displayed, all with tasteful geometric designs, including the newest styles on the Regent shape, patterns no. 12128 (see colour plate XIII) and no. 12132 (see colour plate XII).

Others of the designs which were created that year included Polka Dots, no. 12210; 'graduated blocks', no. 12207; yellow Phlox, no. 12190 (all in colour plate XII); and a pattern simply called Swirls. This was effected by a fine spiral line, applied by brush from the centre and covering the whole surface of the piece in gradually changing

IX Selection of figures by Mabel Lucie Attwell, from 1937

X (a) Teaset and coffee set in Vogue shape, Sunray pattern, 1930

X (b) Dinnerware in Vogue shape, Sunray pattern, 1930

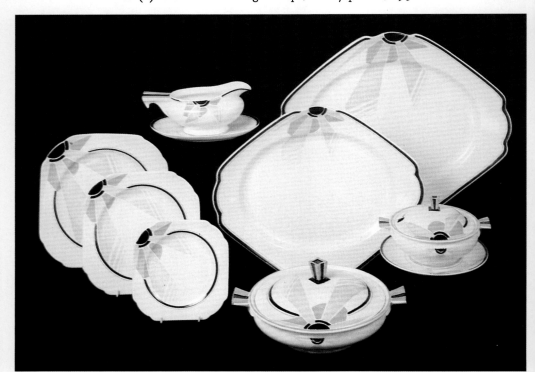

XI Mode shape coffee cups, and Mode and Vogue shape tea-cups in various patterns, 1930

XII Regent shape teaware in various sizes and patterns, 1932-4

XIII Tea, coffee and dinner set in Regent shape, 1933

XIV (a) Tea and coffee ware in Eve shape in bone china, Harmony decoration, 1932
XIV (b) Assorted Harmony Artware, 1932–9

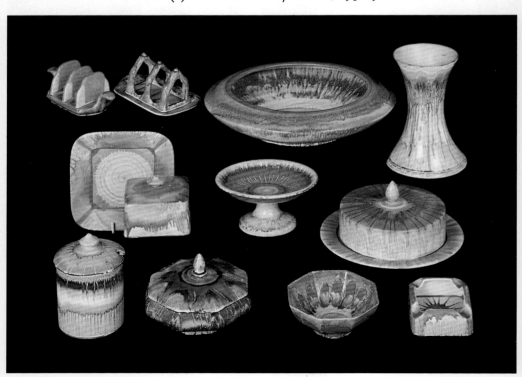

XV Selection of Harmony Artware, 1932–9

XVI Tankards with sgraffito-groundlay decoration by Eric Slater, c. 1951

54 Breakfast set in Swirls pattern on the Regent shape, 1934

colour. Queen Mary, on her customary visit to the British Industries Fair in 1934, was particularly interested in Swirls, and in the geometric pattern no. 12128, and a few days later the firm received a request from the Royal Household to 'submit patterns for Her Majesty's inspection'. These requests were obviously complied with quickly. It is well known that Queen Mary was an enthusiast for pottery, and 'bought' many examples during her visits to numerous stands at these trade fairs, but perhaps she had a special liking for Shelley wares – the following year she purchased two dinner services and an example of Harmony ware, and expressed admiration for a further teaset. The

Princess Royal limited herself to a single Harmony bowl. Even though royal patronage was common practice it did not impress straightforward characters such as Norman Shelley, who had no time for status symbols such as the royal warrant. An apocryphal story regarding Norman relates how one year the Queen on entering the Shelley stand remarked, 'This is a fine display: did I see your firm last year?', to which Norman is said to have replied, 'I don't remember.'

The reputation of Shelley Potteries was steadily becoming more and more substantial through the 1930s, mainly owing to the prestige of their teaware and dinnerware. Eric Slater's standing as a designer was also being more widely recognized. The Society of Industrial Artists, founded in 1930, set up a North Staffordshire branch in 1932: well-known names in art and design such as Susie Cooper and Reginald Haggar were founder members. They organized lively debates on the issue of modern art in pottery design, and were addressed by Chermayeff among others. In 1933 Eric was elected to the committee alongside Susie Cooper, Gordon Forsyth, Colley Shorter (Clarice Cliff's director and, later, husband), Wedgwood's Millie Taplin and Jack Price (designer for Pountney of Bristol and others). Design in industry was very much under discussion at the time even at government level, and when the Council for Art and Industry was appointed in 1934 one of its first investigations was into the education and employment of industrial designers. Eric Slater, with Susie Cooper and Jack Price, was invited to give evidence to the committee, whose secretary wrote to the chairman, 'Mr. Slater has been selected as one of the younger generation of designers. Mr. Forsyth said that he doubted very much whether Miss Clarice Cliff would be of the slightest use for our purpose.' (Gordon Forsyth was no doubt still angry at Clarice Cliff for taking much of the credit for a range of ceramics designed by famous artists of the time, and executed at Cliff's earthenware works.)

In 1935 the S.I.A. branch held a competition amongst its members for original designs. Eric won first prize for a modern styling of dinnerware, with delicate shading at the rim and a very simple motif at the centre. Jack Price took third prize, while Millie Taplin and Susie Cooper were runners-up. Eric's Eve and Regent shapes were also selected that year for inclusion in the important *Survey of British Industrial Arts* by Henry Dowling. The 1930s, therefore, marked the blossoming of Eric's career and his establishment as a distinctive stylist — something he maintained after the 1939–45 war. Looking back on those early angular shapes with a touch of horror, he now regards them as an unsympathetic use of a plastic medium. Nowadays he prefers the flowing curves of traditional wares and the craftsmanship of ornate decoration, although he still has time for his own designs of the 1950s, many of which are as striking as his early works.

The later thirties were rather easier times for china production. As prosperity slowly increased, the fashion for simple designs and the modern banded wares slowly declined. People began to spend money again on decorating their homes and, in response to this, china patterns became more colourful. Some new effects were created on Regent which attempted to simulate the effect of furnishing fabrics, particularly a striped silk effect. Traditional patterns and shapes were sold in increasing numbers. Some of the floral patterns were still bold in their conception but others were introduced with all-over patterns of small motifs in a relatively unimpressive style. One of the most long-standing teaware shapes, Gainsborough, was remodelled as Mayfair, and a series of new shapes was introduced, Oxford, Cambridge, Essex and Kent, all with classical features. In the inter-war period over forty different shapes of teaware are known to have been used, and as a result only the main developments can be recorded here.

A new development, no doubt connected with the rise of public interest in furnishing, was the introduction of Shelley lamp bases and shades in 1937. Two combinations were possible, either an earthenware base with a parchment shade or a china base with a bone china shade (the latter was illustrated earlier in its original commemorative decoration). Either type was available with decoration to match the pattern of tea- and dinnerware, but the lamps were also sold in plain colours to those who were not owners of Shelley china, and in other decorations such as Harmony. A variety of shapes was created, each with its own astronomical name – Orion, Neptune, Jupiter and Virgo.

Harmony Artware was the name given to a large range of hand-decorated, high-fired earthenwares, first produced by Shelleys in 1932. The range initially comprised simple, banded decorations in either graduated shades of one colour or a combination of two shades of colour, one of which was black, which mainly appeared as shades of grey. The aim of these wares was to provide enough variety of colours and shades of colour to complement any colour scheme.

An addition was made to the range by 'a remarkable development' shortly afterwards and trade reviews written at this time found great difficulty in describing the newly developed decoration. 'The design is so original that the effect can hardly be put into words' was one

55 Earthenware lamp bases, c. 1936

account and another stated that 'the colour effects must be seen to be realized'. To many readers, Harmony ware will be familiar, but for those to whom it is not, it speaks for itself in colour plates XIVa, XIVb and XV, which show a representative selection of its later development which is generally known as Shelley dripware.

At first the decoration may appear to be random, but a reasonable amount of skill was necessary to obtain an effective result. The technique used to achieve the dripware decoration was discovered accidentally by Eric Slater whilst experimenting with various colour combinations for the graduated, banded decorations mentioned above. The colour came to the works in powder form and was mixed and suspended in raw turpentine. Different dilutions of the powder-turpentine mixture produced different colour hues. On this particular occasion Eric was using coral red and black: coral red produced colours ranging from red through to orange and yellow; black gave tones of grey ranging from very dark to very light.

The colours were being applied on-glaze and Eric proceeded to apply alternating bands of black and coral red in various dilutions. This was achieved by spinning the vase he was decorating on a wheel and applying the colours to the body with a brush. The turpentine evaporated quickly and as it did so the colours held their position, but Eric stopped the wheel before the turpentine had evaporated fully and immediately the different bands of colour ran downwards, running into one another. Although this was far removed from the effect Eric had set out to achieve, he decided that what had happened was worth investigating. More pieces were produced in an attempt to gain greater control over the rate and amount by which the colours would run and Eric discovered that breathing on to the colours arrested the glaze dispersion. These later trials gave the pots an appearance as though they had burst into flames through their smokey-grey background. The effect was so striking that Eric went on to decorate and fire a number of different shapes in the same way but using various colour combinations.

Eric considered that the effect might have definite commercial possibilities. A length of velvet was bought and draped over some boxes in the packaging warehouse on which the newly decorated wares were displayed. Eric's next move was to ask Percy Shelley to come down to the warehouse to look at the make-shift display, suggesting that what he was about to see could be saleable. Percy was indeed impressed and agreed that the ware might well be worth marketing, provided that the girls in the decorating shops could manage to obtain the same decorative effects without too much difficulty. Eric was certain that, if the glazes were of the right consistency, if the decorator's wheel was stopped at the correct time and if the girls were able to attain a level of breath control, there was no reason why they could not master the technique and produce identical effects. This proved to be the case and, in order to test the commercial viability of the new line, the range of Harmony dripware was taken to retailers in Leeds. Reaction was favourable and sales proved so successful that the new line was quickly reordered. No time was wasted and a consignment was sent down to the London showrooms, and in 1933 the range was exhibited at the British Industries Fair.

The Harmony ware proved to be so popular that it was not long before twenty-five girls were needed to decorate it. Apart from its 'instant appeal' and ability to 'bring a splash of optimism to the table' (according to contemporary trade journals), its success at this time was partly due to its competitive price. It was inexpensive to produce because, in the hands of the skilled decorators, its multi-coloured effects could be obtained quickly and effectively and, above all, it required only one firing after glazing.

Another indication of the popularity of the dripware in particular was the request by buyers for its availability in bone china. This is recorded in the surviving pattern books (which show patterns used on bone china and earthenware dinnerware only). An entry dated November 1932 shows pattern no. 12083 on the Vogue shape in coral red and black (which can be seen on the Eve shape in colour plate XIVa). Pattern no. 12084 in blue and mauve (also shown on the Eve shape) and 12085 in amber and grey have the same date. A later group of colour combinations 12124 to 12127 were entered in February 1933 and applied to Vogue, Eve, Regent and Chester shapes.

Colour plate XIVa, showing the Eve shape in Harmony dripware, appears to show an extraordinary contradiction between the totally ordered geometric shapes and the apparently random nature of the decoration. Despite this, the overall result is extremely effective.

Unfortunately, no documentation on this range of pottery has come to light, apart from references to it in trade journals and two leaflets, one of which lists wholesale prices and the other retail prices. The cover to the wholesale leaflet shows a small group of the dripware in black and white, which is shown in plate 56. The retail leaflet, probably intended for the customer's use, illustrates, in colour, a number of the graduated-band wares. Each leaflet opens out to present a large selection of the shapes available and, between them, 168 different items are listed in sixty-two different shapes, many of which were available in different sizes. For example, vases could be supplied in four or five sizes, flowerpots in six, teapots, coffee-pots, jugs and bowls in four sizes each. These leaflets, however, do not cover the complete range as additions were continually made to supply demand.

Many shapes were made especially for the range and some were available with either a flat or a horizontally ribbed surface. The range was sufficiently large, in terms of shape and colour combinations, to suit most tastes. The Harmony decorations were also applied to earthenwares which had been in production long before their introduction.

56 Harmony ware catalogue cover, c. 1934

Shelley
HARMONY WARE

Even the Art Nouveau candlesticks, one of which is shown in colour plate V, were available in dripware, with surprisingly effective results.

There were two more developments, probably introduced in 1935, in the range which were made by small changes in the decorating methods. One variant of the dripware may be termed 'spot drip', whereby the colour banding appears to have been broken up by dabs of matching colour before the glazes were allowed to run, giving a softer appearance. This type of decoration is shown in colour plate XV on the small, bulbous, ribbed vase in green, brown and blue (top row, third from the right). The other development was the addition of a feathering effect to the graduated-band decorations, usually applied to the tops of vases and jugs or to the edges of plates and other flat ware. One rather curious feature of the bases of much of the range was that they were decorated with a fine spiral in the predominant colour of the piece, almost identical to the Swirls pattern in production on bone china.

Apart from the Shelley backstamp, bases were usually marked either with a one- or two-figure number, or an initial or, occasionally, a group of dots. These were hand-written by the decorator to whom the mark belonged. This was common practice throughout the industry and enabled the decorator of any piece to be identified should there be any errors or, indeed, if the piece was singled out for excellence. Impressed numbers sometimes occur, usually on vases, and these refer to the shape or mould number. Items which were easily described were not impressed in this way because they were readily identifiable by name. Eric recalls that the 'volcano' shaped vase (shown at the bottom right of colour plate XV) was designed specifically for the Harmony dripware range as the straight, sloping sides aided effective glaze flow. The same applies to the 'space capsule' shape (shown bottom centre) and to the 'ice cream cone' shape (shown top left). The earliest impressed number located to date is 920, which appears on the base of the largest version of the 'volcano' vase. This is most likely to have been the first of the new shapes made for Harmony ware. Any earlier mould numbers which occur probably belong to items in production before the range was planned.

Very occasionally, other hand-written numbers occurred, usually of four figures. Sometimes these appeared with additional lettering and these refer to colours and colour combinations, but the four-figure numbers remain a mystery. Those which have come to light are listed in Appendix B.

Several other potters attempted to copy the dripware, but without success. It was firmly believed that Shelleys had developed their own medium to which the powder colours were added, enabling the glaze to behave in the way that it did. The medium, as was mentioned earlier, was simply raw turpentine. Eric recalls how the firm of Johnson Matthey had been requested to supply a Spanish potter with a large quantity of the medium that Shelleys were using. They obliged, sending raw turpentine labelled 'Special Shelley Medium', but at a 'special' price. Eric received a turkey and cigarettes at Christmas for a number of years with a compliment-slip from 'The Suppliers of the Special Shelley Medium'!

The colourful Harmony ware formed a very important part of the turnover at the works when it was produced and undoubtedly helped the company through this difficult decade. Nowadays, the public is bombarded with colour in many ways, particularly since the introduction of colour television, yet much of the Harmony ware retains the impact it must have had in those much less colourful days of the 1930s.

The latter part of this period marked a high-point in Shelleys' reputation as creative potters. They were referred to by reviewers as 'the famous Shelley china firm' and, as the following excerpts from contemporary trade journals show, all features of the company attracted superlatives: 'strikingly original'; 'amazing choice of decoration'; 'superb flawless translucent body'; 'has far outstripped many of the so-called famous pottery names'; 'one of the leading pottery houses in the kingdom'; 'there is not a more efficient pottery house existent'; 'showroom one of the most modern of any manufactory'; and finally 'Shelleys . . . march forward as pioneers'.

However, the public reputation which the firm developed and maintained during the 1920s and 1930s can not be appreciated fully without considering the techniques of promotion, advertising and display which the company used, and which were often just as striking as the wares themselves.

8

Advertising, promotion and display

Since the early days of Wileman & Co., Percy Shelley had been aware of the need to promote effectively his company's products. In those times this had resulted in the manufacture of pottery articles for use in retailers' shops. These included the umbrella stand and advertising tile (illustrated in colour plate II) which were used in various shops to bring attention to the Foley trade name. Other articles of this type included a dog trough for retailers to stand in their doorway, again emblazoned with 'Foley China'.

However, despite the fact that these early advertising techniques were possibly relatively ineffective, as they only reached those people who had already decided to enter a china shop, they were not improved on for many years. During the first two decades of this century, Wileman & Co.'s advertising was very simple, being limited to straightforward listings of the various wares manufactured and other information in a simple traditional typeface. Other promotional efforts seem to have been limited to a couple of showings at British Industries Fairs in the early 1920s.

It was during this period that the influence was beginning to be felt of a man who applied new thinking to pottery advertising and who was to have a considerable effect on Shelleys' image. This man was W. H. Smedley, a native of Stoke-on-Trent, whose fresh thinking was generating considerable interest even to the point of his being an invited speaker to the Ceramic Society.

Smedley's message was simple and the way he expressed it was more so. 'There is no secret in advertising,' he said, 'it is simply a matter of commonsense and truth', but the way he blended these two elusive qualities was far from simple. He was of the opinion that it was far better to sell the commodity rather than the name, and although modern advertising practice would question this separation, at that time the common practice was to focus on a manufacturer's name in a very unsophisticated way.

When Wileman & Co. changed their name to Shelleys in 1925, they also appointed Mr Smedley's agency to handle their advertising. The immediate result was a marked increase in the quantity and quality of advertisements. Shelleys took a full page each month in the most important trade journal, the *Pottery Gazette and Glass Trade Review*, and the themes changed regularly. Smedley kept to his belief in selling the commodity and examples of jelly moulds (see plate 42), decorated earthenwares and Hilda Cowham's nursery ware were featured. The product was given major priority in the design of these pages, with the name of the company taking a prominent but secondary position.

At the same time, coloured illustrated leaflets were produced for each part of the product range and these were distributed to retailers and any postal enquirers. The overall aim, of course, was to bring the public's notice to Shelley wares and to assist retailers in this task. Somewhat unusually for the time, the company soon made this explicit: in mid-1926 they started to advertise their advertising material, and their policy of promoting promotion techniques was to extend considerably in the next four years.

The policy of creating pottery articles for the retailer was maintained with an umbrella stand showing the new trade name. In about 1926, however, this was extended to create in pottery something which was for advertising purposes alone and had no other use – the Shelley Girl.

The Shelley Girl (see colour plate VI) was a china figure standing about 30 cm (12 in.) high and had been modelled by one of the team at Smedley Services. With her paisley design dress, cloche hat, fox fur, and delicately poised cup, she appeared in shopkeepers' displays across the country demonstrating how fashionable and stylish tea-drinking could be, and how much more so with Shelley bone china.

The Shelley Girl theme soon began to spread. She was drawn in the *Pottery Gazette and Glass Trade Review Diary* in the same fashion, taking tea at a small, elegant table, but this time an identity was given to the otherwise anonymous lady: her name, for this advertisement at least, was Elsie Harding. Another version of the now well-established paisley pattern dress graced the cover of a small magazine, called the *Shelley Standard*, which Shelleys introduced in 1927 for retailers and others.

100, showing illustration of rich teaset in colours?

Shelley
REGISTERED
Trade   Mark

57 Detail from an advertising leaflet, 1926

58 Advertising umbrella stand, c. 1926

PLEASE USE.

Shelley China

POTTERS TO THE WORLD

Shelley ENGLAND

59 Shelley Girl
advertisement, 1926

60 Shelley Girl as the
cover to the *Shelley Standard*,
1927

Here, however, the heroine of the piece sacrificed her hat and white fox fur for a much more active pose, raising the Union Jack of quality.

That dress was also made 'real' to the general public in another aspect of the promotion campaign. From about 1928 Shelleys arranged demonstrations of pottery decoration in large stores around the country. These involved one or two girls from the factory working either in a china department or even a shop window, and for the first few years of this enterprise the girls were dressed in paisley dresses.

As a promotional image the Shelley Girl faded from view by about 1930. One of her latest appearances showed how styles had subtly changed in just a few years. Her slightly hazy, 'Hollywood' look with inviting eyes across the rim of a Queen Anne tea-cup introduced a new, slightly seductive dimension to the advertising.

The *Shelley Standard* was produced every two months up to 1931. Although at first it contained items such as short stories on Shelley themes written by Jack's father-in-law, John Nelson, it soon became clear that besides the cartoons, the rather corny jokes and photographs of personalities, this was a vehicle to transmit a set of ideas regarding salesmanship, advertising and display. The company was attempting to persuade retailers to adopt their stance towards promotion, not only by small serious articles on its various aspects but also by using the same advertisements which Smedley had designed, thus identifying the local dealer with the national campaign and image. Enterprising retailers could be supplied with slides for projecting to audiences at the new popular cinemas; printing blocks for the local newspapers; display screens for windows; and a host of smaller leaflets and showcards – even a Shelley doormat! In 1929 the notion of creating other articles to promote the china was extended from the retailer to the customer. In that year Shelleys first arranged with an Irish manufacturer the production of tablecloths to match the decoration on china. These were designed to four of the Queen Anne patterns, of which Blue Iris is the most well known. In 1930 four more were introduced, including Crabtree, but here it seems the series stopped. None of the Vogue patterns is known to have been transferred to linen, and no surviving examples have been located.

Amongst the serious articles in the *Shelley Standard*, and a noticeably large number of items on collecting outstanding debts, humour sometimes shone through. Under the nom de plume Jacques, someone, probably Jack Shelley, demonstrated a zany sense of fun in his 'New Ideas in Salesmanship' which included the advice: 'Always tap the

61 Advertisement for Vogue shape teaware, 1931

THE LATEST FASHION

Shelley CHINA

CALLS FOR A SPECIAL DISPLAY

Link up your Window Display with the Shelley
National Advertising Campaign and enjoy what
is yours—increased sales.

We are prepared to supply you with the Shelley
Dealer Aids which are designed to help you—
leaflets, showcards, price tickets, and special
window display matter.

WRITE FOR A COPY OF THE NEW
SILVER BOOK and further particulars.

SHELLEY POTTERIES LTD,
LONGTON, STOKE-ON-TRENT.

Modern *Shelley* CHINA
WINDOW DISPLAY

62 Example of a window display encouraged by Shelleys, 1931

pieces you are selling in order to demonstrate the ring. As soon as the note is struck, the staff choir will sing "Ring out wild bells" or "Of all the china in the world, the very best is Shelley". A collection could be taken to defray the cost of the annual outing.' Other anecdotes shed light on the economic climate: one retailer is said to have ordered a quantity of leather goods only to receive a telegram from the suppliers sayings 'Cannot despatch your order until the last consignment is paid for.' The retailer replied, 'Unable to wait so long. Cancel the order.'

When the modern Vogue shape was introduced the trade advertising was as striking as the ware itself. Smedley had always recognized that 'the primary thing was always to arrest the eye of the reader'. Anyone reading through the closely ordered pages of the Pottery Gazette would certainly have been arrested by the full-page advertisement illustrated there. The use of space on the page, the typeface and the stylization all led to the main point – Shelley ware calls for a special display.

Through the medium of the Shelley Standard, retailers were shown examples of what the firm regarded as a modern window display. Very effective use of cheap crêpe paper was incorporated, as was a frieze of Mode shapes, to form a modern effect which drew much more attention than the normally cluttered look of a china shop window.

At this time, too, the advertising was extended to national newspapers and magazines on a wider scale, ranging from Punch and Good Housekeeping to the Daily Telegraph and the Radio Times, and reaching a possible circulation of seven and a half million. Part of this advertising suggested that readers write to the firm for a copy of the new booklet which had been produced to illustrate the bone china patterns. Individual leaflets were now a thing of the past, and the first of the new booklets was quite a departure. Called The Silver Book, it bore a silver-effect embossed cover proclaiming 'New Lines of Beauty from the House of Shelley'. Its twenty or so pages illustrated the china all in colour with a variety of geometric forms surrounding the illustrations. This classic Art Deco creation was especially effective in showing the most stylish Vogue and Mode designs, and over a thousand requests per month were received by the firm.

As is no doubt becoming apparent, the cost of these advertising campaigns was increasing considerably, and this at a time when the economic situation was near its worst. Eric Slater put the advertising budget at £10,000 per annum – an enormous amount for those days – and perhaps it is not surprising that this expenditure was not fully covered by profits. Instead, Percy Shelley sold some of a large number of houses he owned in the vicinity of the works and thus financed the promotion (instead of his retirement as was originally intended).

Yet in spite of the depression, the advertising worked. In fact, it worked too well: the number of orders rose steadily, but nothing was being done at the factory to increase the productive capacity. Efficient though the works were, they were not large enough to cope with the demand and the travellers were finding it difficult to keep the store-keepers supplied. The situation grew into one which contrasted cruelly with the anecdote reported in the Shelley Standard: retailers were now cancelling orders because the last consignment had not been delivered by the pottery, let alone paid for by the shopkeeper.

Perhaps this over-stretching of production, together with Percy's retirement, explain why the level of advertising dropped dramatically in 1932. No more full pages in the *Pottery Gazette*, no more issues of the *Shelley Standard*, and no doubt a reduction in press advertising generally – this shows how much the picture had changed. Smedley Services were now only used to design the retail catalogue, something they did with characteristic style: the illustrations were strong and spacious, and showed what alternative colours were available in each pattern; prices were printed on pages which interleaved the illustrations, so that they could be up-dated easily; and the spacing, typeface and colouring was appealing. In 1936 the *Pottery Gazette* took the very unusual step of devoting half a page to review Shelleys' latest catalogue.

Smedley's approach was gaining in popularity: he is known to have worked for a number of potteries, including Susie Cooper, and in 1935 the North Staffordshire branch of the Society of Industrial Artists mounted an exhibition of notable posters produced by Smedley Services. However, the connection with Shelleys was not to last. A disagreement arose in about 1937 between Shelleys and Smedley, concerning the use of the pottery's advertising expenditure; a court case followed, and the two parted company, thereby ending the creative link with a man who believed 'the truth well told constitutes the ideal advertisement', and who produced publicity art well ahead of his times. The effect was noticeable very quickly: the 1938 retail catalogue contained cramped, badly arranged illustrations interleaved with rows of prices and competing typefaces.

One further character needs to be considered when accounting for Shelleys' promotional success in the 1920s and 1930s. This was John Sayer, who ran Shelleys' London showrooms from 1925 but who did not confine himself to simple displays of others' wares. Sayer had had a long connection with the pottery trade and understood the urgent need for improved display. He directed his energy towards creating more effective means of display in showrooms and shop windows.

His first approach was to create stands which would exhibit a complete service of china using a small base area. These 'Ideal Display Stands' were originally wooden pedestal constructions with metal brackets to take the outlying pieces, for example, the 'Tout Ensemble' breakfast set stand. Soon followed the 'Maxima' dinner set stand and then a later series of all-metal one-piece stands, which were designed

63 Detail from one of Smedley's last advertisements for Shelleys, 1936

to give more dramatic, cantilevered settings. The 'Archway' stand was able to range a complete dinner service across the top of an alcove. If John Sayer was attempting to be the Busby Berkeley of china display, then his crowning glory, the 'Uniservice' stand, really matched Hollywood proportions. He had always been of the opinion that every piece in a set should be displayed, but this one stand managed to show four services simultaneously – morning set, teaset, coffee set and dinner set, a total of seventy pieces.

Sayer's other contribution to display was his system of 'Jayesse' fittings. These were made up from vertical slotted strips into which individual fittings could be placed, in a manner similar to later pegboard fittings. Originally made in wood or metal, these were advertised for use in shop windows, but John Sayer had already made more extensive use of them in his own showrooms, where complete walls were fitted with the units, vertical wooden panels filling the spaces between the slotted strips.

There seems to have been a good relationship between Shelleys and Sayer, for not only did the agent often display the pottery's products when advertising his stands, but also the pottery used his stands in their works' showroom and began to use his 'Jayesse' system in their exhibition constructions.

When Shelleys returned to the British Industries Fair in 1933 they began a policy of using their space in a very open way. Rather than creating a building-like construction, as was common for potteries, they arranged their wares on open tables in front of a wall-display at the rear. This caused a great deal of comment, and the following year a much larger stand retained the basic pattern, but the tables were replaced by black glass shelves on tubular chromium supports, and the rear wall was completely furnished with John Sayer's system. Constructed in polished walnut, the background panels provided a vivid contrast for the wares which appeared to float on individual fittings in front of the dark wood. Overall, it was described as 'one of the most striking stands of the Fair'.

A tradition developed of Shelleys and John Sayer taking adjoining stands at the British Industries Fairs, and their combined effort attracted much attention and praise. A 'very outstanding display' was presented in 1935. Perhaps it was the success of these displays which made Shelleys less than enthusiastic over a suggestion of uniform stands for the pottery section of the Fair. Made by the Board of Trade in about 1937, and strongly supported by the British Pottery Manufacturers'

64 John Sayer's 'Uniservice' stand, 1934

Federation, this suggested scheme for uniformity was discussed at great length. It would have sacrificed the individual, outstanding displays of firms such as Moorcroft, Doulton, and Shelleys, for an area of similar displays all promoting pottery as such. On the evidence available, it looks as though Shelleys had not agreed to join such a scheme by the time of their last appearance at the Fair in 1939.

Although the promotion, advertising and display techniques of the Shelley-Smedley-Sayer association extended the reputation of Shelleys' products, that reputation was not built on promotion alone. Shelley china was the envy of many of the better-known potteries, which could of course judge fine china regardless of its promotion, and similarly the buying public were not completely duped by false advertising – they too recognized good china when they saw it. Shelley was a household word which was synonymous with high quality bone china and the promotion aspects merely served to make this truth more apparent.

9
Shelleys' production techniques

In this section some of the special methods the company used to create its bone china will be described. To do this it is necessary to give a brief account of pottery manufacture which will give some insight into the potter's world.

English bone china is composed of three materials: bone, from 35% to 50%; kaolin or Cornish china clay, from 25% to 35%; and china stone – a kind of Cornish granite, from 25% to 35%. Shelleys in fact used up to 52% bone, thus reducing the clay-like properties of the china body, so that it was very difficult to manipulate and handle. The bone was calcined (burned to remove fats and to make it brittle) and ground in water between heavy stones. The three materials were then mixed together with water by various mechanical mixers or 'blungers'.

This created a cream-like mixture called slip, which was suitable for casting but not for throwing on the wheel, so it had to be pumped through filter presses to extract most of the water, and kneaded to the correct consistency in the pug-mill, which also removed any trapped air.

The first stage of potting a plain, round, hollow article, such as a cup or bowl, took place on the potter's wheel. The thrower shaped the cup and polished the inside using a piece of horn. When the article had dried to a leather-hard stage, the turner placed it on his lathe and trimmed, shaved and removed unwanted clay to achieve the particular form, thickness of wall, and shape of foot. The handles, which had been made in plaster of Paris moulds, were fixed on to the ware by the handler, who used slip as an adhesive.

65 Placing the 'green' ware into saggars, using some individual bedders, c. 1930

Flat pieces, such as plates and saucers, were made upside down on a machine called a jigger. The jiggerer threw on to the revolving mould a flat piece of clay called a bat, and pressed down a metal profile of the back of the plate.

Teapots, jugs, fancy-shaped cups (such as Dainty White, Oleander, and Queen Anne), and all articles of irregular shape were cast by pouring slip into plaster of Paris moulds. In a short time the absorption of the plaster deposited a film of clay on the mould and so formed the article.

By whatever technique the piece was made, the ware was at this point called 'green' ware and had to dry before it was ready for its first firing. When fired in the oven, bone china contracts about one-sixth, so that the clay articles were made of sufficient size to allow for this contraction. However, many precautions had to be taken in order to ensure that the contraction was uniform and that the piece did not

66 Creating bungs of saggars in the bisque oven, c. 1930

warp. Shelleys took extra care at this stage: each cup had a grooved clay ring, made by the thrower and turner, placed on to it to prevent it from contracting unevenly. This ring, costing nearly as much in material and workmanship as the cup itself, would of course be thrown away after use. Each plate and saucer was placed in a separate holder called a setter to ensure perfect results. This method reduced the number of plates in each firing by a significant amount; in fact three-fifths of the kiln space was taken up with setters and their associated bedders. All ware was brushed with alumina or flint, to prevent sticking, and was carefully placed into fire-clay boxes, or saggars, before going into the oven. Saggars were made in a wide variety of shapes and sizes, and protected the ware from contamination, flames and gases. They were placed in vertical stacks, or bungs, inside the oven, under the direction of the head placer, known as the cod placer.

The first firing took place in the bisque oven, a brick structure of the famous bottle shape. The outer, bottle-shaped part acted as a chimney and protected the inner part, the actual oven. This was a round structure, with walls approximately 30 cm (12 in.) thick and strengthened by iron bands. A firing took from fifty to sixty hours, about 15 tons of coal were used, and a temperature of about 1,250°C was reached. After two or three days' cooling, the brick entrance (the 'clammins') could be removed and the oven emptied.

At this stage the ware was termed 'bisque' or 'biscuit' ware, and had quite a rough surface. After any remaining particles of flint had been brushed off, the piece of now translucent china was ready for glazing. Applied in a liquid state, the glaze was a form of glass and was spread evenly over the surface by the dipper, with his special, skilled twist of the hand. After drying, the ware was then placed in the glost oven where the firing took about thirty hours and a temperature of about 1,050°C was reached.

When the ware had been carried to the 'white warehouse', it was carefully examined and sorted into complete sets ready to be passed to the decorating department. Losses at this inspection used to run at between 10% and 20%, and would have been considerably higher had it not been for the fact that some minor blemishes could be overcome at the decorating stage. Percy Shelley is reported to have spent much time in the 'white warehouse', ensuring the quality he required and sorting out the ware for the appropriate patterns, details of which he retained in his head.

---

67 *opposite top*: Printers making transfers from copper-plate engravings, c. 1930

68 *opposite*: The decorating shop with teams of enamellers, c. 1930

Shelleys' most well-known technique of decoration on china was that termed 'print and enamel'. Here the outline pattern had first to be engraved on a copper plate by an engraver working from the designer's free-hand originals on a cup, saucer or plate. The engraving was then passed to the printer who applied the ink, laid on thin tissue paper and by passing through a press rather like a large mangle produced a transfer print. This went to the transferer who cut out the required amount of design and applied it to the piece, rubbing down with a stiff brush to ensure perfect contact and finally sponging off the tissue paper.

The enameller or paintress completed the design by filling in with the required enamel colours. These colours were made chiefly from metallic oxides, mixed with various fluxes to enable them to fuse into the glaze when fired. The range of colours was therefore quite restricted and many pottery colours would either not mix with each other or required different treatment and different degrees of heat. The final colour only appeared after the last firing: gold, for example, looked and had the same consistency as black treacle when applied by the gilder. The banded decorations which Shelleys created, and patterns such as Swirls, were executed by the bander, who rotated the piece on a small wheel while applying the enamel with a brush.

The last firing, taking about twenty hours, was in the enamel kiln where the temperature would reach about 800°C. Finally, the ware was taken to the 'papering warehouse' where after a final inspection it was wrapped and packed.

The production of high quality bone china in the 1930s was a skilled and, at times, risky process. The basic techniques were essentially the same as those employed in the Potteries for the previous two centuries, but this outline will also have shown what a labour-intensive process it was, and sets the scene for some of the mechanization and rationalization which occurred in the second half of the twentieth century.

10

The war years, 1939–45, and their aftermath

War was declared on Germany in September 1939. The problems that Shelleys suddenly faced are not to be seen in isolation but need to be viewed in the context of the war's effect on the whole of the pottery industry.

It was soon realized that shortages of labour would have to be faced as a direct consequence of conscription. Materials would quickly become in short supply, bringing inevitable rises in production costs. Initially, however, manufacturers worried about obtaining sufficient work to keep their factories running, but it soon became clear that the greatest problem to be overcome was how to complete orders within a reasonable time. Daylight working had to be introduced which, during the winter months, reduced working hours considerably.

There had, of course, always been two markets to supply, namely the home and overseas markets. The home market was to see many dramatic changes as greater priority was given to exports which earned much-needed dollars. Prices at home were to be regulated by the Government, to curtail profiteering by both manufacturers and retailers brought about by the shortages bound to follow – a lesson learnt from the First World War. The Board of Trade (B.o.T.) introduced china clay control and many clay-pits were closed down. By June 1940 they had limited supplies to retailers to two-thirds of their pre-war level, and six months later this Home Trade Quota was reduced to half. For those companies producing wares solely for the home market, this control was catastrophic, but Shelleys were fortunate in that they had developed healthy export markets before the war began.

Within a short time, the industry was 'concentrated' by the B.o.T. Factory space was needed to carry out essential war work and this meant that some manufacturers had to end production. Only those granted 'nucleus certificates' by the B.o.T. were allowed to continue. Shelleys were granted the necessary certificate and combined their production with Jackson & Gosling, whose works were adjacent. This wartime association involved Shelleys in the production of china dinnerware, not made by them since the early Wileman days, and this was to prove important when peacetime eventually came. Jackson & Gosling was then part of Copeland's and the dinnerware that Shelleys produced was made using Copeland's moulds and decorations. Ovens were shared for fuel economy and at times this gave rise to difficulties between the two workforces, although in general the two teams worked well together. By this time, the younger workers had been either conscripted or transferred to other factories to carry out essential war work, leaving only the older employees to carry on.

The B.o.T. soon not only introduced restrictions on the total amount of pottery produced for the home market, but also imposed severe limitations on the availability of decorated earthenware, which was cut to one-fifth of its pre-war sales in value. However, quota-free concessions were given in respect of coloured bodies and glazes, and of edge and line or $\frac{1}{8}$ in. (3 mm) band decorations on china, although these were quickly withdrawn.

The B.o.T. continued to review the Home Trade Quota and in December 1941 some undecorated earthenware and china were freed from restriction. In February 1942, supplies of decorated pottery were reduced to 15% of their pre-war value and then, on 1 June 1942, in an effort to increase supplies of undecorated ware on the home market, decorated ware was entirely prohibited for the home trade. However, the sale of decorated ware was allowed if it was a reject or part of a frustrated export order. Plain white or ivory utility ware, as it became known, was to be totally quota-free. Manufacture of all other items of domestic pottery was forbidden.

These severe restrictions were met with disapproval and the B.o.T. officials were described as iconoclasts. However, there were those who welcomed the 'Plain White Period'. Gordon Forsyth had deplored beautiful English china badly decorated:

We have had an orgy of 'modern floral', 'period floral', 'rustic floral', 'imitation period' and similar decorations since the last war. The new enforced contemplation of batch after batch of plain, undecorated ware coming from the kilns may have a salutary effect on the Staffordshire Potters. After a period of chaste, virginal shapes, the enormity of some of the pre-war decorations may begin to be realized.

The pattern books reveal that Shelleys were not excluded from Mr Forsyth's criticism of decoration, but it was this kind of decorated ware, it seemed, that some customers wanted. However, not all of the blame was placed on to the manufacturer or customer. Harry Trethowan, managing director of Heal's Wholesale and Export Ltd, and former president of the China and Glass Retailers' Association, strongly suggested that the retailer should take the greatest responsibility; it was the retailer who placed orders with manufacturers and he alone provided the·choice offered to the public.

The Plain White Period, it was suggested, would make manufacturers realize the beauty of their materials, perhaps for the first time. A chain of correspondence was started in The Times by a letter which stated that the introduction of utility wares was seen by some to 'present an unparalleled opportunity to put good design into nearly every home'. Certainly, one of the benefits of the introduction of utility ware was that may people began to consider exactly what was meant by design, good or bad, and the trade journals during the latter part of the war printed more articles than they had ever done before on this subject.

Under directions made by the Board of Trade in the Domestic Pottery (Manufacture and Supply) Order, 1942, utility wares were relatively essential types of plain china and earthenware, and comprised cups, egg-cups, mugs, beakers, plates, saucers, teapots, coffee-pots, jugs, meat dishes and vegetable dishes, sauceboats, cooking ware including pie dishes, bowls, ewers, basins, chambers, hot-water bottles and rolling pins. The articles could be made from a white or light ivory body glazed with a colourless or white glaze. Alternatively, they could be made from a natural clay body, or in the natural colour of the clay with a brown or colourless glaze inside and outside, or with a brown glaze on the outside and either a white or colourless glaze on the inside. Utility pottery was sold in three price grades and pieces were marked A, B or C. Maximum retail prices of a cup and saucer, for example, were as follows: type A, $7\frac{1}{2}$d.; type B, 7d.; type C, $6\frac{1}{2}$d. Shelleys were licensed to produce pottery marked C.

Each manufacturer had his own utility range, so there was a wide choice of shape for the customer, though, by the beginning of 1943, the B.o.T. had imposed restrictions on ranges of objects. For example, there were to be only four sizes of plate and three sizes of cup; saucers were restricted to two sizes. There were restrictions on shape also. If three sizes of cup were offered by a manufacturer, they had to be the same shape. Manufacturers were, however, allowed time to work-off their existing moulds.

The importance of the pottery industry during the war can easily be overlooked but, despite limitations and restrictions, it was considered to be a key industry and was granted an Essential Work Order from the outset of the war. Inevitably pottery has a limited life, estimated to be between three and four years. The most important wartime product was the tea-cup: 150 million were required annually. The process of attaching the handle to the body of the cup is a skilled job and, with the workforce reduced from 66,000 before the war to 25,000, the remaining cup handlers, as they were called, were unable to cope with the demand. The B.o.T. announced that all orders for cups were to include between 10% and 20% handle-less cups, euphemistically called 'Cups in the Chinese Style'. These were extremely unpopular despite suggestions that they afforded a means of fuel economy – people could wrap their cold hands around the cups instead of warming them in front of fires!

Things were brighter on the export market and, provided a company was licensed to export, manufacture for overseas was unlimited. Clearly the U.S.A. and Canada no longer imported from Germany, Japan, Czechoslovakia or Denmark. These gaps needed to be filled and all efforts were made for the British pottery industry to do so; fortunately the North Americans did not impose restrictions on imports from the U.K. On the other hand, British exports were limited, more or less, to Canada, the U.S.A. and the Central and South American Republics.

The majority of the pottery that Shelleys produced for export was traditional in shape and decoration and sometimes highly elaborate. The U.S.A. and Canada, like New Zealand and Australia, had always looked towards Britain for this type of ware and for some time to follow the British pottery industry became almost totally geared to supply it.

War ended on 8 May 1945 and the industry was able to consider seriously its reconstruction, although as early as 1941 the Society of Industrial Artists had shown concern about the end of the war and its consequences. They were worried by the possible loss to the armed forces of young designers, whom they regarded as key people within the industry.

During the war, the British Pottery Manufacturers' Federation had produced three reports on reconstruction and another plan was pre-

pared by the National Society of Pottery Workers. These were all re-
jected by the B.o.T., which in October 1945 formed a working party
for the reconstruction of the whole of British industry, with the intention that the scheme would apply to the pottery industry also.

As soon as the war ended, the Federation requested the release of the
industry from the concentration order. The B.o.T. replied that this
could only be made possible subject to the availability of labour and
premises and, owing to the shortage of labour, it had not yet been
possible to open any of the closed factories. However, by September
1945, the pottery industry was amongst the first to secure the release
of key workers from the armed forces and, by the end of the year, the
B.o.T. had begun to issue licences to companies which had closed
down, enabling them to restart.

Vincent Bob Shelley was not to see the changes to follow and died
suddenly at the age of fifty-one on 29 December 1945. His death left
Percy Norman as sole director and on 7 January 1946 Eric Slater and
Ralph Tatton, the sales manager, were elected to the Board of Directors.
During the war, considerable thought had been given to the rearrange-
ment of the factory, and two major decisions were made affecting the
output of the works. Firstly, it was decided to discontinue the manufacture of earthenware and secondly, since Shelleys had made china
dinnerware to Copeland's designs during the war, it was decided that
it would be a perfectly sensible move to manufacture their own.

The earthenware and china factories were joined together; the
original china works became potters' shops and the earthenware factory
was converted into decorating shops and large warehouses. The new
arrangement formed a continuous flow from the slip-house to the
packaging house. 1946 was to see the installation of Shelleys' first
electric decorating kiln, a Gibson's Rotlec continuous circular tunnel
oven. The Five Towns, familiar to readers of Arnold Bennet, were soon
to change as the coal-fired bottle ovens were replaced by cleaner
electric, gas and oil-fired kilns.

The Council of Industrial Design (now the Design Council) was
formed in 1944 by Hugh Dalton, the then president of the B.o.T., to
promote by all practicable means an improvement in design in the
products of British industry. It was in 1946 that the C.o.I.D. held an
exhibition that was to show the largest selective range of consumer
goods that had ever been seen in the U.K. The pottery industry was
well represented and in the latter part of 1945 manufacturers were
informed of plans and asked to co-operate with the C.o.I.D. by group-

ing together the full range of their own goods and to make them available to the Council's selection committee. Exhibits were to consist primarily of post-war designs: 'Mere copies of traditional or historical pieces would not be of interest although designs based on traditional themes and ideas would be considered.'

The Britain Can Make It exhibition, as it was called, was criticized because it was not intended primarily as an export display, and since decorated wares were still not available, it was thought that the British public would not enthuse over products it could not buy.

Selection for inclusion in the pottery section was made in Burslem in June 1946. No limit was set on the number of items submitted, but intending exhibitors were asked to exercise discretion, realizing the very selective nature of the exhibition and the consequent limitation of space allotted to pottery.

Seven of the designs submitted by Shelleys were selected for the pottery display. All of these, numbered 221–7 in the exhibition catalogue, were designed by Eric Slater, except a 20 cm (8 in.) celadon-ground bowl with a leaf pattern designed by Veronica Ball, an apprentice designer.

The pottery display was under the direction of Harry Trethowan, then display manager to Heal & Sons Ltd. The overall style of the exhibits can best be described as cautious contemporary. The deliberate omission of traditional designs was an anathema to many manufacturers, who failed to see the importance of familiarizing visitors to the exhibition with new ideas. Whatever criticisms were made, amongst the wide range of consumer goods on show, the pottery and glass section proved to be the most popular with the public.

The fourth generation of the Shelley family was represented by Norman's nephews, Bob's two sons: Alan Shelley joined the company in the autumn of 1946 to become sales director, having served in the navy during the war. Two years later, Donald Shelley came to the works to become technical director after graduating in natural sciences at Cambridge.

The company continued to be export-orientated because it was not until 1952 that decorated pottery again became available to the home market. Overseas, Dainty White, decorated with tiny rosebuds or with alternating panels in two colours, emphasizing its petal-like shape, continued to be a best-seller. The advertisement for Sheraton, shown in plate 70 and printed in the *Pottery Gazette* throughout the war and after, shows the type of ware for which Shelleys found a healthy export

69 Dinnerware shown at the Britain Can Make It exhibition, 1946

market. Almost certainly, one of the reasons for the demand for designs which clearly did not belong to the middle of the twentieth century, was the fashion for the 'antique interior', especially in the U.S.A. Today also, it is reasonable to assume that the style of a room will dictate the style and type of pottery used within it.

In 1947 the first British Industries Fair since 1939 was held. This was a major showcase for the pottery industry but Shelleys did not exhibit. There had been a sustained demand for pottery, especially bone china, in the export markets and Shelleys considered it unnecessary to seek orders at home which it could not fulfil. However, changes were made on the export front. Harold Wilson, president of the Board of Trade in 1948, introduced a new type of control. At the request of the British Government, the self-governing countries of the British Commonwealth, namely Australia, Canada, South Africa and New Zealand, imposed import limitations on certain items, but overall these were only on a minor scale. Additionally, the rather smaller exports to the

★ Produced for the Canadian Market in the
true Shelley tradition SHERATON is available in three colour schemes—Green No.
13290 ; Blue No. 13291 ; Pink No. 13289.

For our customers in the Home Market
Shelley White Utility China is available in
as large quantities as we are able to
produce, and we are, as usual, doing our
utmost to satisfy all our customers in these
difficult times.

Shelley
FINE BONE
CHINA

Stockists :
British Ceramics and Crystal Limited, 7, Wellington Street West, TORONTO

Shelley Potteries Ltd., LONGTON, Stoke-on-Trent

70 Advertisement showing a popular example of ware for export during the
Plain White Period

colonial countries were completely prohibited. Although the effects of such restrictions were only limited, any action which led to the possibility of more pottery being exported to dollar countries was considered worth taking. The large loans from the U.S.A. which had helped to finance the war had to be repaid, and the all-important goal was to earn as much hard currency as possible in order to lessen the dollar gap.

'Print and enamel' decorations, so well established at Shelleys in the 1920s and 1930s, were gradually replaced by lithographic and photo-lithographic techniques. Shelleys had always employed their own engraver to produce the copper-plate engravings needed for the print. In the earlier Wileman days, a Mr Mills undertook this work, but between the two wars, when Shelleys excelled in this type of decoration, all of the engraving was carried out by William Cooper. Born in 1873, he joined Shelleys in 1918 and continued to work for them until his death in 1940. Shelleys did not employ another engraver but instead sent any new copper plates to be engraved 'out' by Latchford's, one of the growing number of small firms which specialized in supplying the industry with one particular skill or product. Two designs executed by Latchford's which were particularly successful on the North American market were a range of hunting scenes and a series called English Royal Homes.

The preparation of the copper-plate engravings was highly skilled and took a considerable time, and with more realistic labour costs and the lack of semi-skilled decorators, caused by the disruptive war years, the days of the 'print and enamel' technique were numbered. The sixteen printing teams, consisting of four people in each (printer, transferer, cutter and cleaner), along with the enamellers in the decorating shops, were slowly reduced in number until, in the latter part of the 1950s, they had been replaced by about eighty lithographers.

Concern about designers, their role and number, was to be shown in the pages of the trade magazines, presumably brought about by the Britain Can Make It exhibition and the announcement of the even larger Festival of Britain which was to follow. In 1951, a series of questions relating to design was put to a team of twelve experts by the *Pottery Gazette*. The team comprised R. W. Baker, Professor of Ceramics at the Royal College of Art; Gordon Russell, Director of the C.o.I.D. and ten well-known art directors from the Staffordshire potteries. Eric Slater represented Shelleys and questions put to the panel concerned the training of young designers, the commercial viability of

good design, the specialist nature of pottery design, views on the
C.o.I.D. and modernism in pottery. At this time, within the industry,
these questions were considered controversial and the answers to them
were very varied. Eric Slater, who was then in his fiftieth year, expressed
well-considered and progressive points of view, although curiously he
began to show regret about some of his work with the modernist cubist
designs of the early thirties.

After the war, the British Pottery Manufacturers' Federation realized
that there was a scarcity of designers working within the potteries, and
appealed to manufacturers to make a contribution to the industry by
providing some sort of training facilities for young people who might
be interested in pottery design.

Shelleys were in a strong enough financial position to offer help
and Norman decided to take on several apprentice designers and to
provide them with the opportunity to learn decorating skills at the
works. The company took on about ten apprentices over a number of
years. Each apprentice spent time learning the whole range of decorating techniques by working with and under the instruction of Shelleys'
most experienced decorators. John Heron, the decorating manager,
and Eric Slater were at hand to give advice when needed.The apprentices
spent some of their time 'mending', a term used to describe the hand-
restoration of lithographs which had lifted during firing, and each
week they attended the Burslem Art School for two half-days and two
or three evenings.

Eric Slater recalls that of all the apprentices, Veronica Ball was probably the most outstanding: her work had been exhibited at the
Britain Can Make It exhibition and she was the only named designer
(other than Eric) for this period. Another very talented apprentice was
John Evans, who speaks highly of Norman and states that his willing-
ness to help young people was illustrative of his kind nature. John had
joined the company in 1948 at the age of sixteen but left to do
national service in 1952. During this time, he gained a place at the
Royal College of Art (it was unusual in those days for the R.C.A. to
recruit from industry – the usual way of entry was via an art school),
where he went immediately after his national service. John returned to
the works on completing his course in London but soon realized that
his prospects with the company were limited and left to work for
Chromo-Litho Ltd.

The lithographers began to play an increasing role in the design of
patterns used by the industry. Art directors did less of their own design

work and became more involved in the choosing of patterns submitted to them by the many lithographers who employed their own design teams. Sometimes the art director would suggest modifications to the submitted design and these were happily made. Lithographers still, of course, printed designs sent to them by art directors because often their own designs were inappropriate and out of keeping with a manufacturer's product.

Shelleys' china was selected to be shown at the Festival of Britain, which was intended to mark the centenary of the Great Exhibition of 1851. The original idea for the Festival was put forward in the last years of the war but more definite discussions began in 1947 and, because of the success of the Britain Can Make It exhibition one year earlier, the Government announced that the C.o.I.D. was to be involved with a considerable part of the organization.

The Festival was, above all, to be a selective exhibition. The Britain Can Make It exhibition had shown that such an event was possible; it was popular with the public and manufacturers were willing to submit wares for competitive selection.

Shelley china was shown in four pavilions. In the Minerals of the Island building, under the section on silica and limestone, the bowl shown in plate 71 was exhibited (H 536). In the Power and Production pavilion, Shelleys demonstrated pottery decoration (O 515) and three tableware designs were shown: Mountain Ash (S 562), Vernon (Y 805)

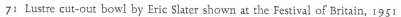

71 Lustre cut-out bowl by Eric Slater shown at the Festival of Britain, 1951

72 Dinner plate and soup bowl shown at the Festival of Britain in 1951 and
illustrated in *Design at the Festival*

and Carlisle (Y 806). A number of blue and maroon jars were shown
in the Homes and Gardens section and in the Lion and the Unicorn
pavilion two more examples of tableware were on view: Summer Rose
(K 530) and Idalium (K 543). (The numbers following each item
are those under which they were listed in the exhibition catalogue.)

As well as the exhibition on the South Bank in London, a travelling exhibition was mounted which visited Manchester, Leeds, Birmingham and Nottingham, and Shelleys were represented here in the 'Best Room' of the People at Home section by exhibiting a lustre bowl and a series of jars (D 854 and D 855). In addition to this, there was the Festival ship, the *Campania*, which sailed to ten ports around the country, with twelve place settings of Idalium on display in the dining-room.

The C.o.I.D. decided that a pictorial card index of all the products selected for the Festival should be compiled. This was termed the *Design Review* and thirty-six of Shelleys' designs were included in it. There was also an illustrated review of British goods called *Design in the Festival* and one of the illustrations from the small section on pottery was of a Shelley design and is illustrated in plate 72. The shapes are traditional in form – Shelleys were not to introduce new shapes for some time to come – but the decoration is unmistakably contemporary. ('Modern' was not a term used to describe the up-to-date designs in the 1950s but referred to the geometric cubist forms of the early 1930s, typified by the Vogue, Mode and Eve shapes and patterns.) The totally free-hand stylized leaves, feathering, dots, cross-hatching, spirals and repeating ampersands could be reproduced effectively and commercially only by the use of lithographs. It is interesting to notice that Susie Cooper used similar themes in much of her pre- and post-war work, and also that she too turned to lithographic techniques.

11

Modernization and take-over

1952 showed a decline in the overseas markets, and primarily for this reason and to avoid unemployment in the industry, some decorated pottery was allowed on to the home market. Hotels and restaurants had preference in the distribution of supplies and the catering trades were allowed to order 'badged and monogrammed ware'. This was considered to be helpful to the tourist trade and thus would indirectly help to earn the much-needed dollars.

Manufacturers had had twelve years of abnormal conditions, shortages of operatives and materials and, during the war, little or no opportunity to replace old or install more modern equipment. Shapes and patterns had to conform to the requirements of foreign customers and it was suggested that it was not good for the potters to have to rely entirely on the whims and fancies of overseas buyers. Also, never before in the long history of the industry had there been so much governmental control.

However, there were advantages to the limitations imposed on the home market. Good prices could be obtained for rejects and seconds, and output was increased because fewer patterns and shapes were made, enabling longer production runs. Business was good in that everything made was sold.

1951 was a bumper year for exports of china. Indeed, since the end of the war in 1945, sales abroad had continually increased. Exports decreased from 1952 to what was termed a slump around 1957, but although the heights of 1951 were not reached again until the 1960s, in terms of pre-war performance, generally speaking the 1950s were reasonably bright.

Nevertheless, the domestic potters had steadily lost ground to other industries – toilet ware to sanitary ware, teapots to the metal trade, hospital ware to stainless steel and glass, and dinnerware in heat-resistant glass was becoming accepted by the public as an alternative to pottery. Plastics had made inroads into the sales of many items. The plastics industry had developed rapidly in the pre-war period and had undergone enormous expansion during the war. On the one hand, the relatively simple mechanized processes of production cost much less, but on the other, the cost of the raw materials was high. Plastics may indeed be unbreakable but pottery offers a much better resistance to scratching and staining, and decorations are much more durable, as well as suitable, on pottery.

After the war, however, these developments outside the industry only affected Shelleys to a small extent, because only bone china was being produced. Bone china has a unique appeal despite its high cost and, even today, its qualities have still to be met by alternative materials. Furthermore, after the war, china sales increased more rapidly than sales of earthenware. With this general background, Shelleys' decision to concentrate on bone china production would appear to have been the correct one.

Price control was removed from most types of ware in June 1952 and, by August of the same year, all controls on the supply of decorated pottery to the home market were lifted. However, the industry again had to face competition from other markets as import restrictions were also lifted. By this time, Japan had reasserted itself and began once more to supply its main pre-war markets, North America and Australasia. Germany, too, was in the market again and many of the wares produced for export were unmistakably contemporary. These proved to be tremendously popular not only on the continent but particularly in the U.S.A. The Scandinavians took a lead in terms of new ideas and style and became a great influence throughout the design field. Additionally, because of shortages, countries which had previously imported pottery began to manufacture their own wares.

The prosperous years immediately after the war had lulled the industry in Britain into a false sense of security. The majority of Shelley wares produced at this time were traditional in shape and decoration and related to eighteenth- and nineteenth-century design. Such wares produced in the post-war years can not be considered to have made a valuable contribution to the pottery industry other than providing much-needed employment and the financial means by which new ideas could be expressed. Less representative wares, however, were also available, some of which are discussed here.

Despite the need for less labour-intensive, and hence cheaper, decorating methods, in 1952 Shelleys announced that they had revived a combination of two types of hand-decoration using sgraffito and groundlaying techniques for small-scale commercial production.(The shortages of lithographs at this time may have been partly responsible for this.) Sgraffito in this instance referred to the technique of scratching through a thin layer of colour (rather than slip or glaze) which was applied by a groundlay method. Groundlaying is essentially an on-glaze decoration involving coating the article with a thin layer of oil to which colour in powder form is applied. Areas which are to remain uncoloured are covered with a solution of sugar and water by brush, sometimes through a stencil, before the oil coating is applied. Shelleys' combination of these two types of decoration enabled finer detail to be obtained than was possible by the application of the sugar and water solution, which would have been used only to mask larger areas. The tankards shown in colour plate XVI were all decorated using this method. All the patterns produced were designed by Eric and, on the wares made available commercially, vine and ivy leaves, decorative tendrils and cross-hatching were common themes. Additional hand-painted decoration was kept to a minimum and often was not required.

It is reasonably certain that most of Shelleys' contemporary patterns which had been exhibited at the Britain Can Make It exhibition and at the Festival of Britain were decorated using these techniques, with additional hand-painting. These designs were mostly experimental and Eric's interpretation of 'contemporary', and it is likely that they were done with the Council of Industrial Design, an organization Eric admired and understood, in mind. Their commercial viability was considered uncertain and these new designs were usually described as being 'for possible future production'. Some of the designs called for less elaborate shapes, although Eric must be congratulated on having made the most of the shapes available to him at the time, and it is interesting to note the frequent use of the bowl in its simplest form. Exhibition pieces have always tended to be either 'one-offs' or limited editions, and this appears to be the case for Shelley ware also.

The Burslem School of Art, founded in 1853, became the headquarters of the Stoke-on-Trent College of Art when this was formed in

73 Lustre bowls by Eric Slater shown at the Burslem School of Art Centenary, 1953

1952. Its centenary was celebrated by an exhibition of pottery and paintings by former students and teachers, both past and present. The object of the exhibition was to show the changes in technique, style and thought that had occurred since the School's inception. Amongst the 184 pieces of pottery exhibited, ten designed by Eric were shown, thus illustrating how highly regarded he had become within the industry.

The constraints imposed by the war and the limitations during its aftermath were followed by many changes and undoubtedly the most important ones were technological. Marketing, packaging and retailing were to change as were people's lifestyles, with influences such as television having an impact on domestic habits. New shapes and patterns were called for as an increasing number of people became more design-conscious. Although it is not within the scope of this book to discuss all the technological changes that took place within the pottery industry, it is of interest to see how Shelleys decided to cope with some of them. Too often, the end-product is viewed without any consideration of the processes which give rise to it. There are great benefits for those seriously interested in pottery in familiarizing themselves with the manufacturing and decorating techniques. The technology involved need not be tedious and it throws a stronger light on the merits, or otherwise, of the resulting product.

Several changes were made at the works after the war. In addition to the new layout of the buildings and the installation of the Rotlec decorating kiln in 1946, a Gibson's electric truck kiln was installed in 1950 and used to fire glost ware. (The ware was wheeled in and out of the heating chamber using trucks on rails.) This particular kiln was chosen by Donald Shelley, who was to show a growing interest in the development of electric kilns. The new kiln increased the rate of production of china dinnerware as well as reducing losses. Donald's interest in the technical side led him, in 1952, to begin work on a cup-casting machine which was operational six months later. It remained in use until 1967.

The greatest change on the manufacturing side, not only for Shelleys but for the whole of the industry, was the gradual replacement of the coal-fired bottle ovens by kilns fired by oil, gas or electricity. The bottle ovens had served the industry for two hundred years and were wasteful of heat, costly to run in terms of labour and fuel, and notorious for the filth they produced in and around the potteries.

The continuously firing tunnel oven, in which trucks carrying the items to be fired were slowly moved through the firing sequence, was an alternative to the bottle ovens. The first successful tunnel oven, developed by Conrad Dressler, was in use in 1910 and was fired by coal. If fired by gas, oil or electricity, it was considerably cleaner and, if run to full capacity, more efficient and cheaper to run. However, the tunnel oven was costly to buy and install. It did not lend itself to small batch productions, a requirement Shelleys felt they needed. Something less expensive and more flexible had to be devised and Donald Shelley decided to solve some of these problems himself. He approached Mr Scholefield, of the Midlands Electricity Board, who suggested that Shelleys should build a small, experimental, intermittent, electric truck kiln for china biscuit firing.

In 1953 Shelleys had purchased adjoining buildings, which had housed Jackson & Gosling's works, and the following year, in one of these, the experimental kiln was constructed with Mr Scholefield providing the electrical expertise and Donald Shelley handling the mechanical side. Six months later, another biscuit truck kiln, based on this prototype, was built in the china works. Donald then proceeded to

74 Donald Shelley with one of the 'Top Hat' kilns

design and build two electric decorating kilns, again of the truck type, which were also installed in the china works adjacent to the Rotlec kiln. At this stage, most of Shelleys' biscuit ware was still being fired in five bottle ovens.

Donald Shelley then took an interest in the 'Top Hat' kiln, a type of kiln which the company decided to develop itself, and a prototype was in operation by the middle of 1955. With these kilns, the unfired wares remain in position whilst the kiln itself is lowered down to cover them. Firing then takes place and, after a cooling-down period, the 'Top Hat' is removed. Shelleys decided to commit themselves fully to this type of kiln for the biscuit firing, and in late 1955 a one-storey building was constructed on the site of a previously demolished boiler house to house the new kilns.

By the early part of 1956 four 'Top Hats' were in operation and accounted for about 70% of the biscuit firing. The remaining biscuit was fired partly in the prototype truck oven and its successor and partly in some of the coal-fired bottle ovens.

Before the war, traditionally each pottery had processed all the raw materials that formed the constituents of the body, made its own glazes, developed and made its own equipment and constructed its own kilns. In May 1956, Shelley Potteries formed a subsidiary company, Shelley Electric Furnaces Ltd, with Norman, Alan and Donald Shelley as directors and with Shelley Potteries holding 70% of the shares. As the post-war period saw the development of specialist supporting industries, Shelleys' decision to continue to build their own kilns would appear to be against the general trend. It is probably more accurate to describe this move, in which the research and development costs must have been high, as a diversification, because Shelley Electric Furnaces Ltd were in the market to manufacture and sell their kilns.

By the end of 1956 eight 'Top Hats' and sixteen bases had been constructed in the new building and these met all of the biscuit firing needs. Shelleys' bottle ovens were at last obsolete, and in 1957 numbers 3 and 4, which were at the back of the works, were demolished to provide a workshop for the manufacture of the 'Top Hats'. Even the prototype truck oven was no longer needed and was eventually dismantled. Each 'Top Hat' could fire three times a week: one day was needed for the heating-up and another day for the cooling-down. The old bottle ovens, though having a large capacity, had taken five days, 15 tons of coal and considerable labour. The intolerable working conditions experienced by some of those involved in the firing sequence of the bottle oven and the extraordinary skills and responsibilities demanded are recorded in an accurate account prepared by the City Museum, Stoke-on-Trent, and the Gladstone Pottery Museum. The last bottle oven firing was carried out by the Gladstone Pottery Museum in 1978.

In 1963–4 major modifications were made to the layout of the works. The potting shops were moved from one of the old three-storey buildings into three single-storey bays. Another of the old three-floor buildings, also at the back, made way for these and the demolishing and rebuilding was done in two stages, in order to cause minimum disruption to production.

Shelley Electric Furnaces, having supplied Shelley Potteries with all the kilns they were to need, had begun constructing kilns for other manufacturers, but changes were needed here also, when the converted buildings being used were found to be inadequate. Most of the Jackson

& Gosling's site had been demolished in 1954 and this land was used for new premises for the furnace company. These were built in 1960 and an extension was added in 1964: two years later, however, Shelleys fired their last pot.

As soon as restrictions were lifted in 1952, the potters had to decide what the buying public would want. For twelve years the home market had been starved of decorated ware and a generation had grown up familiar with only plain utility wares. Would they seek traditional shapes and patterns, would they want something fresh and contemporary or would they play safe and go for a combination of the two? There would, of course, be a market for all types of ware, but it was not known which would prove to be the most popular and commercial.

For Shelleys, this problem was not acute because 80% of their output was being exported to markets they had developed and already knew. Before the war, exporters had used the home market as a testing ground for their new designs. Those which sold well at home usually sold well abroad. Was this approach still appropriate or indeed might its converse be true? With these considerations in mind and with the knowledge that new shapes and ranges required considerable outlay and an element of risk, Shelleys decided to market at home the traditional shapes and patterns with which they had found success overseas. New patterns, traditional in character, were introduced and some of the pre-war traditional shapes were revived with the addition of some new shapes for tea and coffee ware, reminiscent of nineteenth-century styles. The newly introduced bone china dinnerware produced when the war ended complemented the traditional tea and coffee sets popular overseas (see plate 69). Note the shape of the dinner plate, tureen and soup bowl; although the coffee-cup's 'can' shape may appear to be more modern, it was in fact in use in the eighteenth and nineteenth centuries. Some of the shapes produced were identical to the dinnerware produced at the works before the 1914–18 war. For a number of years, though, a team of four people decorated wares, mainly tea and coffee sets, using the sgraffito-groundlay technique and their work did offer a taste of the contemporary, although it was very much a compromise in that their shapes, too, were traditional. The team did, however, allow some scope for experiment.

It is important to point out the differences between the marketing of bone china and earthenware. Bone china is considerably more expensive to produce and buy and is therefore usually bought to last. As a result there has always been a tendency for it to be restrained in

its design – contemporary designs sometimes date very quickly. Earthenware, because of its relatively lower cost, can exploit new trends much more readily and with less financial risk. This is not to say that contemporary designs did not occur on bone china – Shelleys' intro- duction of the Vogue, Mode and Eve shapes during the early thirties bears witness to this. They were totally up-to-the-minute, even futur- istic, when they were first introduced, but they did date and lose their appeal rather quickly. Fifty years later, this work is seen in a very different light and these modernistic designs, rather than fading into obscurity, have become one of the high points of style from the era in which they were produced. However, the 1930s and the 1950s do not bear comparison. The economic and social climates were totally differ- ent and, for Shelleys, motives and personalities had changed.

Many of the designs exhibited at the Britain Can Make It exhibition and at the Festival of Britain did not go into production. Shelleys were not yet prepared to branch out into the contemporary field. Some manufacturers complained that designs which won awards were not commercial, whereas patterns based on posies, Windsor Castle and horses and hounds sold well, particularly abroad. For some reason, buyers from other countries looked to England not for contemporary designs but for traditional ones.

The war may have been partly to blame for this, in that it had stopped any innovation, and there were the technological changes the industry had to face. The Plain White Period, the dollar drive and even the post- war boom had all been unimaginative, despite encouragement from the Council of Industrial Design. British potters were slow to introduce new shapes and over-cautious, but this is not to say, by any means, that the British potters did not respond at all to the call for new ideas at home and abroad or take risks in introducing new shapes and patterns. In the forefront in earthenwares were Midwinter, Poole Potteries, Wedgwood and, of course, Susie Cooper, some of whose pre- war work may indeed be termed visionary. Eventually, by the mid- to late 1950s, all British potteries, including Shelleys, responded.

The 'look' of the fifties, for pottery, was unmistakably a combination of 'T.V. screen' and free-form shapes, together with streamlining. However, some critics of these streamlined designs suggested that pottery should not appear as though it were about to break the sound barrier. Fitness for purpose provided a guiding line and some of the

75 *opposite top*: Bowl of experimental design by Eric Slater, sgraffito-groundlaid with additional brush strokes, c. 1954

76 *opposite*: Experimental design by Eric Slater, sgraffito-groundlaid with additional brush strokes, 1955

Victorian flamboyancy, still evident, was purged. To some extent, pottery reflected the social changes that occurred in the fifties. The big increase in new housing during this period meant that more people were living in modern surroundings, and this would have had some effect on the demand for contemporary pottery.

One important development was brought about by the revival and popularity of the coupe shape in America in the early fifties. 'Coupe' was the term used to describe the rimless plate. The rim is the traditional resting place for salt, pepper and mustard, and for some its absence was too much to bear: 'where else could one possibly put one's condiments?' In 1953 it was suggested that 'this type of plate might even be demanded in the U.K.!', and by 1955 many manufacturers had realized that the popularity and demand for this new shape was as significant here as it was in America.

In the autumn budget of 1955, 30% purchase tax was imposed on pottery sold at home. This was an attempt by the Government to restrict United Kingdom consumption, which, it was hoped, would provide pottery manufacturers with an incentive to increase their exports. This was far from welcomed by manufacturers, however, who had begun to invest in new shapes specifically for the home market. Shelleys were less affected by this large tax than most potteries because of their policy to remain export-orientated. The popularity of these new shapes did, however, lead to Shelleys' plans for their first post-war contemporary shape and, by the end of 1956, it was in production. This was called Stirling and was designed by Eric Slater and modelled by Alan Forester. One of the most attractive patterns used on it was Fantasy, which is shown in plate 77. Stirling was a coupe shape and was available in tea, coffee, breakfast and dinnerware. It was important to make a full range available because, in the U.S.A. particularly, a fully co-ordinated look to a table setting was important and one of the reasons for purchasing something new. The introduction of a coupe shape filled a very obvious gap in Shelleys' post-war output: the company was again making a contribution to developments in new designs.

The development of a new shape was an empirical process. Eric would present outline sketches to the modeller, who would translate them into a three-dimensional form using clay or plaster of Paris. There would be a discussion about the prototypes and any modifications considered necessary would be made at this stage. Plaster of Paris moulds would be made from the results, enabling tests to be carried out on the practicability of manufacturing the shape. If there

77 The Stirling coupe shape with the Fantasy pattern, 1956

were any difficulties, the modeller would begin again. The whole process would be repeated if cups or pots did not fire to the size required to hold a certain amount of liquid.

A similar procedure would sometimes be used by the art director with pattern design. He or she would present one of the most skilled decorators with drawings and the decorator would 'paint them up' on to the appropriate shape. Any modifications, if needed, would depend on how successful the two-dimensional design appeared on the three-dimensional object.

During the late fifties, the Queen Anne shape was reintroduced for a short while, having been discontinued after the war. Two entries to the pattern books of this time illustrate how important it is for a pattern to relate to and complement the shape to which it is applied.

The Fantasy pattern was used on both the Stirling shape, with which it was totally complementary, and on the Queen Anne shape, on which it was highly inappropriate. All potters make mistakes and Shelleys were no exception.

Though Shelleys may be accused for having been late with new shapes, it was usual within the bone china trade for a time lapse between the introduction of a new style in earthenware and a similar one in bone china. If a new shape, introduced in earthenware, proved popular and successful over a reasonable period, then the bone china manufacturers would risk the high cost of introducing their own interpretation of it. This illustrates that no pottery manufacturer operated in isolation and each company took a keen interest in what others were doing. If you were good enough and lucky enough to introduce a successful shape, you inspired others; if you failed to do so you were inspired by someone else who did.

Mabel Lucie Attwell ware was still being produced and under her married name of Mrs Earnshaw, although now well into her seventies, she continued to submit drawings for Shelleys' consideration. However, the nursery ware was made in much smaller quantities than in the pre-war days. Sales were restricted by its high price; it was three times more expensive in bone china than its earthenware equivalent. The printer made a high charge for drawing-up new subjects on their lithographic stones, although, if the print order was large enough, this charge could be waived. Such large print orders had become too great for Shelleys' needs, however, and this led to their suggesting to Mrs Earnshaw's agents that another manufacturer might be approached to produce Mabel Lucie Attwell ware in earthenware using the same transfers. The cost of the large, but more economic, print runs could then be shared. Simpsons (Potters) Ltd of Cobridge were approached in June 1956, on Shelleys' recommendation, and they agreed to co-operate. By September, samples of their own range of nursery ware had been produced and were marketed soon after. It is interesting to note that Shelleys did not find any decrease in the sales of their china series, as might have been expected because of the introduction of the much less expensive range offered by Simpsons. This is a good indication of how different the markets for bone china and earthenware were at that time.

In 1956 the last British Industries Fair was held in London. After the war, it had become so large and all-encompassing that it was felt that smaller specialist trade fairs would be more suitable. For this reason,

Shelleys did not exhibit at the Fair after the war but chose instead, as did other potteries, to show at the International Gifts and Fancy Goods Fair, first held in Harrogate and, from 1956 onwards, in Blackpool. By 1957 this had become the principal showcase for the industry.

During the fifties, new ideas for patterns used more and more colour, clearly in reaction to the Plain White Period, and black was used frequently to give greater emphasis to both strong and pastel colours. The use of sketches on pottery had also become popular in contemporary design. Eric had always maintained that there was a close link between fabric design and the patterns used on pottery. Two fabric designs popular during the fifties were 'Gingham' and 'Polka Dots', and these patterns soon appeared on pottery produced by many manufacturers. Shelleys used small polka dots, available only in red, blue, turquoise and green, on one of their traditional shapes and, later, on the Stirling coupe shape. One manufacturer featured, in one of its advertisements, a woman wearing a dress with large polka dots, pouring tea from a matching teapot into a matching cup and saucer on a matching tablecloth. This totally co-ordinated look is a little confusing; it is not easy to see who and what is where.

Such extremes as these were matched by lines produced for the large and important bridal market. Shelleys' Bridal Wreath, Trousseau and Bridal Rose patterns on Dainty ware remained ever popular. The prettiness of these designs appealed very much to the mothers and aunts of brides-to-be: it must have been hard luck if you were a bride-to-be who was mad about polka dots.

In 1959 the Stirling shape was shown at the Design Centre, which had been opened in the Haymarket in 1956, and Evergreen and Pastoral were the names of the two patterns placed on view. Although Eric recalls that the success of the Stirling shape was limited, it is interesting to note that, with the Fantasy pattern, it became very popular in Sweden. At this time Shelleys had agents in twenty-seven countries.

The Council of Industrial Design was beginning to be recognized as influential and this was not popular with many manufacturers who disliked the increasing role played by it. There were fears that the public would assume that if a product was not displayed in the Design Centre or not included in the Design Index, it was bad design.

It is convenient to review the recent past in terms of decades, although this sometimes gives the impression that, suddenly, everything changed on moving from one into the next. This is of course far from the case; one decade is born of another and changes are usually gradual. However, people take stock of events as a new decade begins and it was clear that what had been happening in the late fifties was to set the scene for the future. For many, certain events were unsettling as changes were made within the industry, and even more unsettling as changes were brought about by outside forces. It was becoming clear that the strength of the industry was moving away from the many small, family firms into large public companies. The industry was contracting, in terms of its number of independent manufacturers, a result of mergers and take-overs. Changes in themselves were not new, but in the past they had tended to be dictated by family size and strength. Marriages had sometimes brought about mergers, and families had increased the size of their works as the size of the family increased, and sold off existing works as the size of the family decreased. The nature of the changes was very different during the fifties and sixties, and the reasons for them are many. The industry had developed because of enterprising family businesses, many of which had been established in the eighteenth century. Until the beginning of the Second World War, labour had been plentiful and cheap, but after this time, sharp increases in wages and the cost of fuel and materials meant that firms were forced to mechanize. In addition to this, new marketing methods were needed. These necessary changes were beyond the resources of many small firms.

The development of the large company is best illustrated by the interest taken in the potteries by the large and powerful financial holding company S. Pearson & Sons Ltd. Its chairman, Lord Cowdray, whose sister had married the London agent of Booths Ltd, had provided financial assistance to Booths in the 1930s. Later, in 1944, Colclough Ltd, another Stoke-on-Trent pottery, was acquired. Then, in 1952, the Lawley group was taken over. This consisted of a chain of glass shops and the factories of Ridgways and Swinnertons in Stoke-on-Trent, which had been acquired by Lawley's in 1945.

In 1964 Pearson's decided to augment its interests in pottery and the large and successful Stoke-on-Trent firm of Thos. C. Wild & Sons (manufacturers of Royal Albert china) was purchased. Also in 1964 the Royal Crown Derby Porcelain Co. Ltd was acquired, which added to the prestige of the new group. It was now in a position to supply a full range of fine bone china and earthenware. In the same year, the name Allied English Potteries was adopted to cover all the Pearson group's interests in the pottery industry.

At this time Pearson's were undoubtedly a major external force. Some mergers, amalgamations and take-overs had taken place within the industry during the fifties but this greatly accelerated during the sixties. The development of Allied English Potteries may have been a catalyst – a necessary one, because of the very definite signs that the industry was changing from being craft-based to being science- and technology-based. Such a change demanded either the injection of new capital or at least the pooling of resources. Developments in kilns and other equipment had been an early indication of this technological change but two announcements made in 1960 must have made it even more clear. The first was the announcement by Royal Doulton that they had developed and intended to use a totally new body called English Translucent China. E.T.C., as it was known, was china without

78 Tea and coffee ware in the Avon shape with the Mosaic pattern, 1965

bone and could be produced for half the cost of bone china, mainly due to the greatly reduced firing times required and because of lower wastage. Although its qualities were not as high as those of bone china, they were close to it. Secondly, in 1960, W. T. Copeland & Sons Ltd announced that they had developed a new non-translucent ceramic body with strength and durability superior to any other tableware body then currently in production.

1964 appears to have been a watershed with not only the Crown Derby take-over but with Wedgwood's bid for W. T. Copeland & Sons Ltd. Although the latter eventually proved to be unsuccessful, both these events shook the pottery industry.

Such was the background of events against which Shelleys and other potteries found themselves placed during the early part of the 1960s. Perhaps it was this background which led to the development of a new style with much less flamboyant shapes than some of those from the fifties. Curves were replaced by straight lines and patterns became more restrained.

In January 1965 Shelley china made its first appearance at the trade fair held in Atlantic City in the U.S.A. Alan Shelley attended the show and the complete range was exhibited in conjunction with the firm's distributors, Shelley-Walker Ltd. It had become clear that agents alone were insufficient and a more direct approach to sales was needed. In the same year, Shelleys introduced what was to be their last new shape. It was called Avon and was available in the full range of tableware. The Mosaic pattern on this shape is illustrated in plate 78.

In May 1965 Shelley Potteries Ltd were renamed Shelley China Ltd. It is curious that this change had not been made earlier, since Shelleys had been producing only bone china for twenty years. The following year proved to be a sad one, not only for the family but also for the company. In May, Norman Shelley died at the age of seventy-two, and three months later, Allied English Potteries acquired Shelley China Ltd and Shelley Electric Furnaces Ltd.

Many small firms were unable to undertake the expensive modernization necessary for their survival. Shelleys had achieved more than many by developing the 'Top Hat' kiln and improving their works, but the resulting loss of liquidity may have been partly responsible for the eventual take-over. At the same time, however, Allied English Potteries felt the need to expand its bone china output and clearly the skilled workforce at Shelleys, together with the reputation it had maintained, made the company an attractive proposition.

Epilogue

The story of Shelley Potteries would seem to have come to a natural close in 1966 when the company was taken over. Certainly the family's connection with the china works came to an end at that time. The factory was very quickly turned over to the production of Royal Albert bone china, its name became the Montrose Works, and it seemed that the Shelley name would disappear completely from the world of fine china manufacture. However, it was not long before some observers, including directors of Allied English Potteries, recognized that the demise may have been too hasty, especially in the American market where Shelleys' reputation was strong.

In 1971 Allied English Potteries merged with the Doulton group, so that Shelley became one of many names in china production which that group owned. The company Shelley China Ltd still in fact exists: nil returns are filed with Companies House each year.

During the last stages of the preparation of this book, it has been discovered that Royal Doulton may be considering using the name again, and that trial wares have been produced bearing the Shelley mark. It appears that this book, therefore, rather than recording a completed episode in pottery history, may merely describe one phase of Shelley china, and it would seem that future collectors may now direct their attentions to Shelley wares which are yet to be produced.

Appendix A: Backstamps

1872–90

1890–1910   Variants incorporate the names Urbato, Spano-Lustra, Faience, Semi-Porcelain and The Foley China

c. 1912–25   The words Late Foley were incorporated 1910–c. 1916

1910–c. 1925 on heraldic miniatures

1925–c. 1945   The words Fine Bone China were added 1945–66

1930–32 on china

1936–7 on commemoratives only

Appendix B: Pattern numbers

Dating Shelley china from pattern numbers

Each piece of Shelley china carries a painted number on its base along with the backstamp. This is the pattern number and refers to the applied decoration. With the aid of the list given below, the year in which any pattern was entered into the pattern book (and thus the year when a particular piece was probably first produced) may be ascertained. The pattern books were rationalized in 1919 and only the books since that date have survived, so that the few dates given before 1919 have been found by other means. After 1919 the first pattern number in each year is given.

No.	Date	No.	Date	No.	Date
3744	1888	11600	1928	13100	1940
5045	1891	11648	1929	13297	1942
9333	1896	11717	1930	13626	1946
10037	1905	11818	1931	13842	1956
11000	1919	11936	1932	13891	1957
11152	1921	12115	1933	13935	1958
11218	1922	12267	1934	13969	1959
11254	1923	12361	1935	14021	1960
11321	1924	12446	1936	14070	1961
11386	1925	12591	1937	14127	1962
11454	1926	12683	1938	14180	1963
11538	1927	12880	1939	14227	1964

(last pattern = 14288)

When the same pattern was applied to more than one shape, a reference letter for the shape would precede the number painted on the piece. These letters included:

A. Gainsborough   P. Vogue
D. Vincent   R. Mode
F. Low Queen Anne   U. Eve
G. Tall Queen Anne   W. Regent

When the same pattern was available with different colour backgrounds, a reference letter or number for the colour would follow the painted number, after an oblique dash. Thus U 11754/31 denotes a 1930 pattern, applied to the later Eve shape, and using the colour denoted by number 31 (a bright yellow).

By far the majority of pattern numbers encountered will be of the five-figure variety. However, there are a few examples of numbers in a different format, for example W 058 or CS 078. These refer to special patterns, often intended for the export market, or for a particular customer. Some are also accompanied by a small backstamp which states 'Ideal China No. . . .'. Ideal China was a slightly less expensive version which Shelleys produced in the 1930s.

Pattern numbers on earthenware

Little information is available regarding pattern numbers on Shelleys' earthenware products as no pattern books are known. Sometimes an earthenware piece carries two painted numbers: one of these will be of three digits and refers to the shape, while the other will be of four digits and refers to the applied decoration. Thus 773 8262 refers to the vase in plate 36 with the Indian Peony pattern; 793 8660 refers to the vase in the centre of plate 48 with Moorcroft-style decoration; and 786 8356 refers to the small round vase in the top row of colour plate V with lustre butterfly decoration and pink interior. A selection of the known pattern numbers is given below to aid collectors in identifying those decorations which have not been illustrated. All dates are approximate. Virtually no information is available on the shape numbers and they rarely appear on the wares.

No.	Pattern	Date
7821	Blue snakeskin effect	1901
7919	Cloisello	1914
8035	Moiré Antique	
8103	Roself	1916
8178	Violette	
8251	Carnation	1917
8262	Indian Peony	
8306	White fish lustre	
8315	Blue Dragon	

No.	Pattern	Date
8318	Vinta lustre	1919
8320–1	Cloisonné	1920
8334	Madame Butterfly on black	1921
8356–7	Lustre butterfly, various interiors	
8365–6	Madame Butterfly on yellow, mauve	
8504	Roself, later variety	
8660	Moorcroft-style	1929
8718–9	Moresque	1930
8727	Tulip motif on black	

8769–72 ⎫
8779   ⎪
8792   ⎬ Harmony   1932
8823   ⎪
8827   ⎭

Appendix C:
Registered design numbers

As well as backstamps and pattern numbers, some pieces of Shelley china and earthenware bear a registered design number which may be useful in identifying a particular piece. This number denotes that the shape or the pattern was officially recorded and was protected against copying under various Acts of Parliament. The year when a design was registered is not necessarily the first year in which that design was produced; some were only registered when they proved popular. Over 250 designs are known to have been registered by the Shelley pottery in its various phases: some important ones are given here.

No.	Date	Design
6559	1884	Teaware shape, hexagonal body and handle
60650	1886	Teaware shape, ribbed body
64761	1887	Commemorative pattern, Queen Victoria's Golden Jubilee
92158	1888	All-over transfer pattern in blue
115510	1888	Cup and saucer, scalloped shape
175636	1891	Ivyleaf border pattern
272101	1896	Dainty White shape teaware
290929	1896	Commemorative pattern, Queen Victoria's Diamond Jubilee
330274– 330309	1898	Intarsio and Urbato (including 330278– 80, grotesques)
336411	1899	Intarsio umbrella stand
363131	1900	Character teapots, including Lord Salisbury
397890	1902	Nursery rhyme transfers
594382	1912	Oleander shape teaware
468736	1905	Wild rose pattern
633218	1914	Cloisello pattern
637802	1914	Moiré Antique pattern
651677	1915	Decanter (pattern by Frederick Rhead?)
657617	1916	Violette pattern (similar to Roself)
663447	1918	Bryta nursery ware

No.	Date	Design
669655	1919	Bedpan
673709	1919	Vinta lustre pattern
674954	1920	*Cloisonné* pattern
681788	1921	Bubbles pattern
709687	1924	Hilda Cowham plates (first series)
721559	1926	Mabel Lucie Attwell plates (first series)
723404	1926	Queen Anne shape teaware
724421	1926	Mabel Lucie Attwell teapot and sugar-bowl (mushroom)
726181	1926	Mabel Lucie Attwell milk-jug (Boo Boo)
731977	1927	Hilda Cowham plates (second series)
742953	1929	Queen Anne shape coverdish
756533	1930	Vogue shape teaware
781613	1933	Regent shape teaware
795072	1934	Oxford shape teaware

Appendix D:
A chronology of the firm

1860	Foley China Works built by Henry Wileman, alongside his Foley Potteries
1862	J. B. Shelley joined the firm as a traveller
1872	J. F. Wileman took J. B. Shelley into partnership, to form Wileman & Co.
1881	Percy Shelley joined the firm
1896	Frederick Rhead appointed as art director
	J. B. Shelley died
1898	Works expanded to include earthenware production
1905	Walter Slater appointed as art director
1910	Trade name changed from Foley China to Shelley China
1918	Percy's three sons, Norman, Jack and Bob, joined the enterprise
1919	Eric Slater started to work with his father, Walter
1925	Name changed to Shelleys
	Smedley Services took over the advertising, John Sayer became the London agent
1929	The limited company Shelley Potteries was formed
1932	Percy Shelley retired
1933	Jack Shelley died
	Frederick Rhead died
1937	Percy Shelley died
	Walter Slater retired and died soon after
1939	Firm 'concentrated' with Jackson & Gosling
1945	Bob Shelley died
1946	Bob's two sons, Alan and Donald, joined the company
1956	Shelley Electric Furnaces Limited formed as a subsidiary
	'Top Hat' kilns installed
1965	Name changed to Shelley China Ltd
1966	Norman Shelley died
	Company taken over by Allied English Potteries

Bibliography

Journals

Pottery Gazette (later the Pottery Gazette and Glass Trade Review)
Pottery and Glass Record
Artist (especially 1896–1900)
Art Journal (especially 1905)
Studio (especially 1896–1903)
Yearbooks of Decorative Art (especially 1954–5)
Cox's Potteries Annual
North Staffordshire Chamber of Commerce Yearbook

Other publications

Aslin, E. & Atterbury, P., Minton 1798–1910, HMSO/Victoria & Albert Museum, 1976
Atterbury, P. & Irvine, L., The Royal Doulton Story, Royal Doulton Tableware Limited, 1979
Battersby, M., The Decorative Twenties, Studio Vista, 1969
Battersby, M., The Decorative Thirties, Studio Vista, 1971
Betteridge, M., Royal Doulton Exhibition 1979, Sydney Museum of Applied Arts and Sciences, 1979
Blacker, J. F., The ABC of Collecting Old English Pottery, Stanley Paul & Co., 1910
Bunt, C. G. E., British Potters and Pottery Today, F. Lewis, 1956
Council of Industrial Design, Design 46, HMSO, 1946
Council of Industrial Design, Design in the Festival, HMSO, 1951
Dowling, H. G., A Survey of British Industrial Arts, F. Lewis, 1935
Eyles, D., Doulton Burslem Wares, Barrie & Jenkins, 1980
Forsyth, G. M., 20th Century Ceramics, Studio Publications, 1936
Gay, P. W. & Smyth, R. L., The British Pottery Industry, Butterworths, 1974
Godden, G. A., Victorian Porcelain, Herbert Jenkins, 1961
Hawkins, J. & Hollis, M., Thirties, Arts Council of Great Britain, 1979
Jewitt, L., The Ceramic Art of Great Britain, Virtue & Co., 1878
Packer, A., Mabel Lucie Attwell; a centenary exhibition, Brighton Museum, 1979
Rhead, G. W., The Principles of Design, Batsford, 1905
Rhead, G. W., British Pottery Marks, Scott Greenwood & Son, 1910
Rhead, G. W., Modern Practical Design, Batsford, 1912
Rhead, G. W., The Earthenware Collector, Herbert Jenkins, 1920
Rhead, G. W. & Rhead, F. A., Staffordshire Pots and Potters, Hutchinson & Co., 1906 (reprinted 1977, by E.P. Publishing)
Scarratt, W., Old Times in the Potteries, privately published, 1906
Williams, T. G., Social and Industrial Change 1870–1924, Pitman, 1925
Yass, M., Britain between the World Wars 1918–1939, Wayland, 1975

Index

Abrahams, R. F., 27
Adams, Harvey, 17, 53
Advertising techniques, 114–15, 118, 120–2, plates II, VI, 57–64
Advertising ware, 88–9, plate 44
Allen, Thomas, 27, 30
Allied English Potteries, 160–1, 162, 163, 171
Arms china, 66, 69, plates 30, 31
Arnoux, Leon, 26, 27, 28
Artist, 24, 30, 37, 40
Ashbourne pattern, 60, plate 27
Ashtead Potters, 83
Atlantic City Trade Fair, 162
Attwell, Mabel Lucie, 80–5, 158, 170, plates VIIIa, IX, 38, 40, 41
Avoine, Maxime, 24
Avon shape, 162, plate 78

Bailey, Margery, 78, 85
Baker, Prof. R.W., 141
Ball, Veronica, 138, 142
Belleek Pottery, 54, 72, 79
Birks, Rawlins & Co., 47, 79
Board of Trade, 124, 133, 134, 135, 136, 137, 139
Bodley, E. J. & Sons, 27, 53
Bone china, 78, 127, 147
Booths Ltd, 160
Brain, E. & Co., 52, 98
Bretby Pottery, 39
Britain Can Make It exhibition, 137–8, 141, 142, 143, 148, 155, plate 69
British Industrial Art Exhibition, 1920, 64
British Industries Fairs, 64, 73, 104, 109, 124, 126, 139, 158
British Pottery Manufacturers' Federation, 97, 124, 136, 137, 142

Brown-Westhead & Co., 25, 53
Brownfield, W. & Sons, 27
Brownfield Guild Pottery, 28
Bryta nursery ware, 80, 169
Burslem School of Art, 63, 142; centenary, 148–9
Bursley ware, 47, 49, 75, 79

Campbell, Colin Minton, 27
Cauldon Potteries, 47, 49, 53
Character teapots, 34, 169, plate 9
Chermayeff, Serge, 104, 106
Chicago Exhibition, 1893, 22, 54
China and Glass Retailers' Association, 135
China dinnerware, 22, 61, 137, 153, plate 69
China manufacture, 21, 127–8, 130, 132
City Museum, Stoke-on-Trent, 16, 152
Cliff, Clarice, 98, 106
Clock cases, 33, plate III
Cloisello ware, 59, 71, 167, 169
Cloisonné pattern, 73, 75, 168, 170
Coates, Wells, 104
Colclough Ltd, 160
Coleman, W. S., 30, 32, 43
Commemorative wares, 69, 71, 169, plates 32, 33
Cooper, Susie, 106, 122, 145, 155
Cooper, William, 141
Copeland, W. T. & Sons Ltd, 27, 49, 134, 137, 162
Council for Art and Industry, 106
Council of Industrial Design, 137, 141–2, 143, 145, 148, 155, 159
Cowham, Hilda, 80, 82, 170, plates VIIIb, 39

Dainty Floral, 24, 96
Dainty White shape, 24, 69, 138, 159,
    169, plate 4
Daniel, John, 25
Daniel, Ralph, 25
Design and Industries Association, 104
Design Centre, 159
Design Council, see Council of
    Industrial Design
Dinnerware: china, 22, 61, 137, 153,
    plate 69; earthenware, 95, 101, 102,
    plates Xb, 53
Display techniques, 122, 124, 126
Domestic ware, 85
Doulton, Burslem, 54, 56, 59, 78, 85,
    126
Dresden Works, Longton, 17
Dressler, Conrad, 150

Elden, Matthew, 23
Elkin, Knight & Co., 18
English Translucent China, 161
Evans, John, 142
Eve shape, 101, 145, 155, 166, plates
    XIVa, 52, 53
Exhibition of Industrial Art, 1933, 104

Fenton School of Art, 25
Ferneyhough & Adams, 17
Festival of Britain, 141, 143–5, 148,
    155, plates 71, 72
Flambé decoration, 59
Flamboyant ware, 57, 59
Foley, 18, 52
Foley backstamp, 52–3, 164
Foley China Works, 19, 20, 64, 171,
    plates 14, 29; earthenware extension,
    22, 37; other extensions, 39, 64,
    152, 171
Foley Potteries, 18, 19, 20, 39, 171,
    plate 2
Forester, Alan, 156
Forester, Thomas & Son, 49
Forsyth, Gordon, 63, 101, 102, 104, 106

Gainsborough shape, 60, 75, 107, 166,
    plates 27, 36

Gildea Pottery, Burslem, 27
Gladstone, W. E., 28, 34, 53
Gladstone Pottery Museum, 15, 28, 152
Gladstone Testimonial Vase, 28
Goss, W. H., 66
Grotesques, 39, 169, plates 15, 16
Groundlaying, 148

Haggar, Reginald, 106
Hammersley, Doris, 78, plate 37
Hammersley Pottery, 83
Hanley School of Art, 22, 63
Harmony ware, 107–10, 112–13, 168,
    plates XIV, XV, 56
Hartshorne, Samuel, 17
Heraldic china, 66, 69, plates 30, 31
Heron, John, 142
Hill, Oliver, 104
Hospital ware, 88, 170
Hürten, C. F., 49

Ideal china, 167
Indian Peony pattern, 75, 167, plate 36
Intarsio ware, 29–30, 32–4, 37, 57,
    169, plates I–IV, 5–9
International Gifts and Fancy Goods
    Fair, 159

Jackson & Gosling, 23, 134, 150,
    152–3
Jahn, Louis, 28
Jelly moulds, 85, 88, plates 42, 43
Jewitt, L., 17, 19

Kauffer, E. McKnight, 104
Kilns, 19, 130, 137, 150–2
Knight, Clara, 97, plate 49
Knight, John King, 18, 52
Knight & Wileman, 18

Lamp bases, 107, plate 55
Lane Delph, 16
Lane End potteries, 15
Latchford's, 141
Lawley group, 160
Lithographic decorations, 75, 80, 94,
    141

Longton, 15, 18, 19, 51, 91
Lustre glaze wares, 72–3, 167, plates V, 34

McGrath, Raymond, 104
Manufacturing techniques, 127–8, 130, 132, plates 65–8
Mappin & Webb, 59
Micklewright, F., 22
Midwinter Ltd, 83, 155
Mills, Mr, 141
Minton, Hollins & Co., 54
Minton's, 22, 25, 26, 27, 28, 29, 30, 32, 41, 47, 53, 54; Art Pottery Studio, 23, 43
Mode shape, 98, 99, 101, 102, 145, 155, 166, plates XI, 50, 51
Moiré Antique pattern, 62, 167, 169
Moorcroft, William, 96, 126, 167, 168, plate 48
Moore, Bernard, 23, 34, 59
Morris, Rowland, 22–4

National Art Training School, 22
National Council of the Pottery Industry, 65
National Society of Pottery Workers, 137
Nelson, Eileen, 78, plate 37
Nelson, John, 118
New Hall Pottery, 25
Newcastle-under-Lyme School of Art, 25
Noke, Charles, 56
North Staffordshire Chamber of Commerce, 52, 65, 91
North Staffordshire Liberal Federation, 65
Nursery ware, 80–5, plates VIII, IX, 38–41

Oleander shape, 60, 169
Oriental influences, 59, 60, 71, 72, 73–5, 76
Oxford shape, 107, 170

Paragon China Ltd, 83, 98
Parian, 23, 41, 69
Pastello ware, 29, 37, plate 13

Pâte-sur-pâte, 26, 27, 28, 29, 37, 47
Pattern books, 30, 166–7, plates 5, 50
Pearson, S. & Sons Ltd, 160–1
Pinder, Bourne & Co., 54
Plain White Period, 134, 135, 155, 159
Plastics, 147
Poole Potteries, 155
Pottery and Glass Record, 25, 49, 83
Pottery Gazette, 22, 47, 49, 75, 78, 82, 101, 115, 121, 122, 138, 141
Pottery Managers' and Officials' Association, 47, 65
Price, Jack, 106
Primitif ware, 29, 37
'Print and enamel' decoration, 94, 102, 132, 141, plates 67, 68
Protât, M. Hughues, 22

Queen Anne shape, 93–6, 157, 158, 166, 170, plates VII, 47

Regent shape, 102, 104–5, 166, 170, plates XII, XIII, 54
Rhead, Frederick Alfred, 25–30, 32–4, 37, 39, 40–1, 43, 47, 49, 65, 75, 171, plates I–III, 5–13, 15–20, 23, 25; his brothers, 27, 30, 41, 43, 47, plates 21, 22; his children, 49; his early family, 25, 53
Ridgway's, 53, 160
Roself decoration, 62, 168, plate 28
Roumana lustres, 73
Royal Albert china, 160, 163
Royal Crown Derby Porcelain Co., 160, 162
Royal Doulton, 161, 163
Rozenburg wares, 30
Russell, Gordon, 141

Sayer, John, 79, 122, 124, 126, 171, plate 64
Sgraffito decoration, 34, 41, 148, plates 10–12, 18; sgraffito-groundlay, 148, 153, plates XVI, 75, 76
Shelley, Alan, 138, 152, 162, 171
Shelley, Bob, 61, 63, 77, 137, 138, 171, plates 37, 46

Shelley, Donald, 138, 150, 152, 171, plate 74
Shelley, early family, 15–17
Shelley, Jack, 61, 63, 77, 92, 171, plates 37, 46
Shelley, Joseph Ball, 17, 18, 19, 21, 22, 171, plate 1
Shelley, Norman, 61, 63, 78, 106, 137, 138, 142, 152, 162, 171, plate 46
Shelley, Percy, 21, 22, 50–1, 52, 65, 89, 91–2, 121, 171, plates 45, 46
Shelley, Pye & Company, 17
Shelley & Adams, 17
Shelley & Hartshorne, 17
Shelley backstamp, 52, 53, 164
Shelley China Ltd, 162, 163, 171
Shelley Electric Furnaces Ltd, 152, 162, 171
Shelley Girl, 115–18, plates VI, 59, 60
Shelley Potteries Ltd, formation of, 92
Shelley Standard, 115, 118, 120–1, plate 60
Shelley-Walker Ltd, 162
Shelleys, name of firm, 79, 171
Shorter, Colley, 106
Showrooms in London, 20, 22, 79
Simpsons (Potters) Ltd, 158
Slater, early family, 53, 54
Slater, Eric, 63, 97, 106–7, 108–9, 137, 138, 142, 148, 149, 156, 159, 171, plates XVI, 49, 71, 73, 75, 76
Slater, Kenneth, 97
Slater, Walter, 53, 54, 92, 171, plates IV, V, 24, 25, 49
Smedley Services, 79, 114–15, 118, 120–1, 122, 171, plates VI, 42, 56–7, 59–63
Society of Industrial Artists, 106, 122, 136
Solon, Louis M., 26, 29, 47
Spano-Lustra ware, 29, 34, 73, plate 10
Spode, Josiah the younger, 16

Spode Ltd, 16, 41
Staffordshire Pots and Potters, 43
Stirling shape, 156, 158, 159, plate 77
Stoke School of Art, 22, 26, 63, 148
Surrey Scenery ware, 57, 59
Survey of British Industrial Arts, 106
Swinnertons, 160
Sydney Museum of Applied Arts and Sciences, 54

Tablecloths, 118
Taplin, Millie, 106
Tatton, Ralph, 137
Toilet sets, 59, plates 17, 26
'Top Hat' kilns, 151–2, 162, plate 74
Trethowan, Harry, 135, 138
Turner, William, 16

Universal Exhibition, Paris, 1878, 27, 47
Urbato ware, 29, 34, 169, plates 10–12
Utility wares, 134, 135, 153

Vincent shape, 94, 166
Vinta lustres, 73, 168, 170
Vogue shape, 98–9, 101, 145, 155, 166, 170, plates X, XI, 61

Wedgwood, Godfrey, Clement and Lawrence, 27
Wedgwood, Josiah, 15–16
Wedgwood, Josiah & Sons Ltd, 26, 27, 47, 98, 155, 162
Wedgwood Institute, Burslem, 23, 28, 53
Wild, Thos. C. & Sons, 23, 160
Wileman, Charles J., 19
Wileman, Henry, 18, 19, 171
Wileman, James F., 19, 20, 21, 171
Wileman & Co., formation of, 21
Wilson, J. S., 23
Wood & Sons, Burslem, 47, 49, 75, 79